Best wish

OUTDOOR JUNKIE

from Robin Huth

by
Robin Huth

Canadian Cataloguing in Publication Data

Huth, Robin.
  Outdoor junkie

  Includes bibliographical references.
  ISBN 1-55212-404-5

  1. Outdoor life--Anecdotes. I. Title.
GV191.6.H87 2000   796.5   C00-910697-9

Published by Wombat Press
Silverton, British Columbia

Printed by Office Depot
Richmond, British Columbia

Pre-published anecdotes

ACKNOWLEDGEMENTS

This book has come alive through the efforts of a few people besides myself. I gratefully acknowledge the patience of Betty Carlson, a fellow British Columbia writer, for her perceptive and frank assessments. My wife, Dorothy, by questioning the use of a word, the turn of a phrase, the position of a paragraph, by her probing and suggesting, and who lived the outdoor life with me, is as much the author of this book as I am.

I am grateful to those rangers who gave me their perception of ranger travel, and family life in the bush, and I'm thankful that I knew such iron men as Howard Schlorff, Larry Erickson and Rocky Morin.

PREFACE

Outdoor Junkie delves into a tiny portion of history — a story that ended two generations ago. There is history in the portrayal of the old-time trapper as he mushed behind his dog team, taking a week or more to get around his trapline. Had he been presented with a snowmobile, he might have looked askance at the noise and smell of the contraption.

There is a history in the travels of the old-time forest ranger. The lifestyle and method of transportation of the first ranger changed not at all in some provinces from the beginning of forest ranging in the 19th century until the 1950's. He relied on his horse to get around his district, or sometimes a homemade raft or a dog team. Now the ranger is a specialist. He has moved to town, and he has traded his horse for a truck.

The old-time timber cruiser, following his compass needle through bramble and bush, across muskegs and over hills, bears no resemblance to a man sitting in a drafting room, computing timber volume by peering through a stereoscope at an aerial photograph of a forest.

We must not forget these old-time bushmen, their work and life. This is history, and history must be handed down from generation to generation.

**

In context with the period in which most of the book has taken place, the author has used Imperial measurement throughout.

TABLE OF CONTENTS

ONE

HUDSON'S BAY FUR TRADE

"Don't let no one steal yer dreams."

On a sunny day in June 1938, I stepped onto the gangplank of the S.S. Keenora. The aroma of tar, hemp rope and wood smoke from her boilers added to my excitement. I was 17 years of age. Soon, crewmen winched up the anchor, the ship's whistle emitted an ear-piercing blast, and we shoved off from the wharf.

It had all begun a week before when the postman had pushed a letter through the mail slot in the front door of my parent's home. On the top left corner of the envelope was the Hudson's Bay Company's logo! I knew intuitively that it held good news – the Company had accepted my application as an apprentice fur trader.

I had often thought of Silas O'Hara's advice. Silas, the neighborhood's all-round roustabout and handyman, could roll a cigarette with one hand, and he could spit tobacco juice with unerring aim at any target he selected.

"Don't let no one steal yer dreams," he said. "A young man who hesitates is lost."

My mother didn't want me to hear this philosophy. I was hoping the company would send me to the Arctic. Her idea of an outdoor adventure was to pick the roses in the garden, and she used to shake her head at my yearning to live in the bush. "The babies must have got mixed up in the hospital when you were born," she said, "you couldn't have come from me."

On the other hand, my father encouraged my urge to get into the wilderness.

My upbringing hadn't prepared me for life in the bush. Brandon, Manitoba, during the 1930's, was small enough that a boy could get out to the fields to mess around in the sloughs and water-filled ground depressions in the early spring. During the summer, he could take some old blankets, and walk down the railroad tracks to spend a Saturday night beside an aspen lined creek. This was nice, and even adventuresome, but it was not wilderness, and as I matured, so did my desire to see what the north held for me.

The Keenora was to take me 200 miles north on Lake Winnipeg to the Berens River Indian settlement. There I was to report to the Company's trading post factor. As a clerk and trainee, my salary was $25 a month with board and room.

Only three passengers were on board besides myself: two young nuns not much older than me and an Icelandic fisherman.

The S.S. Keenora, with her afterdeck full of firewood for her boilers, and her bridge resplendent with a uniformed captain, plied her way between Winnipeg and Norway House at the top of the lake, taking a week for the round trip.

The S.S. Keenora

(Years later, I took another jaunt on the Keenora, this time with my bride. It was summer and every cabin on board was filled. The passengers danced on her open deck to music from an old upright gramophone. When the Old Dame blew Her whistle, everyone stopped dancing, and held their hands to their ears to close out the piercing bellow.)

But now, it was early spring. The ship was on its first trip of the season, and with only four passengers, the journey was quiet. I stood in the bow watching the broad expanse of water spread out until the last view of land faded. Whitecaps had formed, and the ship gently rolled and bucked against marching grey and green swells. Presently we came to the first of many islands. The Keenora's whistle signalled to a village of Indians that she would take on some of their stacked firewood for her boilers. When we tied up beside a flimsy wharf, the ship's navvies laid out the gangplank, and dozens of Indian dogs on shore set up a howl from their tethers. A gang of bronzed braves hustled over to throw logs into the bowels of the steamship.

As I lay in my bunk that evening looking out of a porthole at the sun's dying rays, a large vee of Canada geese aimed itself in the direction the ship was going. Their wild honking called to me. *This is what I have been looking for! Can it be really happening?*

About noon the next day, we sailed into the little settlement of Berens River situated on a wide, crescent shaped bay rimmed by a sandy beach. Along the shoreline were a number of buildings, most of them small log cabins from which smoke drifted lazily skyward. Along the beach, a few hundred yards from the cabins, were three larger buildings: the Hudson's Bay trading post, an RCMP detachment, and a huge log inn. The Keenora's whistle signalled a sudden throaty blast, causing the passengers to jump, before carefully pulling alongside the company's massive wharf.

From the wharf a well worn path led to a one story white building with a red roof. A large sign over the door proclaimed this as the *Hudson's Bay Company, established May 2, 1670.* Almost the entire settlement met the boat. I had to push past chattering, excited native men, women and children to get to the company's store.

I introduced myself to the dour Scot behind the counter.

Almost with reluctance, the post manager offered his hand. His only other acknowledgment of me was to say, "I'll be at the wharf seeing to the freight the boat brought in. You can keep busy by sweeping the floor. There's the broom over there."

I hadn't expected this. I had impressed on the two young nuns a somewhat romantic view of the duties of a fur trader. Their first sight of me with a broom in my hand would take away from the effect I had been trying to achieve. Perceiving them approaching the store, I threw the broom over the counter, and met them at the door, and with a proprietary air, showed them around.

An Indian dressed in black denim pants and a blue work shirt stepped through the door. Seeing me behind the counter, he approached and said something in the Saulteaux language.

The two nuns looked at me expectantly.

This was my chance to take charge, and show I was an intrepid fur trader.

But I had no idea what the man wanted.

"Er, the manager will be here shortly," I said lamely. The Indian broke into a volley of words that meant nothing to me. He pointed to a small box of short, black, thin sticks. While I was pondering on how I could end this one sided discourse with dignity, the prettier of the two nuns said, "He wants you to sell him some tobacco."

I looked at her in surprise.

"They are those long, black sticks in the box. People up here call them niggerheads."

"How do you know?"

She smiled sweetly. "Oh I'm fluent in the Saulteaux language. My father was an independent trader at Island Lake, and I was raised with the Indians."

To my relief, the post manager came back at that moment, and the women left almost immediately to return to the ship.

That evening I walked over to meet the mounted policeman, Corporal Cyril Calcraft, but he was away on patrol. The police office, jail, and living quarters stood a few yards east of the Hudson's Bay Company. It was staffed by one man whose beat encompassed hundreds of square miles of lakes, rivers and forests. When Calcraft was on patrol, his resourceful Austrian wife, Pearl, chopped wood for the home fires (unless there was a prisoner to do it for her), fed the prisoners and fought the loneliness.

On the night I met her, she was ironing one of her husband's shirts with a "sad iron". Taking immediate control of the conversation, Pearl directed it towards her physical toughness and strength. "I can cut down a tree as good as any man," she informed me in her Austrian accent. Rolling up her sleeve, she said, "Feel my muscle." I gingerly squeezed her bicep, and was disconcerted to find it was larger and harder than my own.

Some weeks later, I experienced my first forest fire. An Indian "tripping" to a wilderness lake had seen the tell-tale column of smoke above the trees, and raced to give the alarm. The initial spark had come to life several miles inland. No one knew how it started, but it may have been by lightning.

The fire created a great deal of activity around the trading post as men from the settlement prepared to fight it. The Forest Service had cached its equipment, ready for action, in the back of the company's store. Groups of Indians ran in and out of the store bearing Wajax back pumps and other fire fighting tools. The trading post's manager and I packed grub for the men to take to the fire. When they had equipped themselves, they left singly and in groups.

Soon the people at the settlement were hearing stories of wind-tossed pieces of flaming wood igniting new fires in the dry moss and pines a mile ahead of the advancing fire line. The fire seemed to be out of control.

I wondered how the natives and the few whites in the settlement would get along if they lost their houses.

I thought of Ma Kemp. Her inn was all she had. The loss of it would devastate her as she relied on tourists and commercial fishermen for her living. Dubbed years later by a newspaper reporter as "the unquestioned Queen of the North," Ma was a warm, big hearted woman who held court in her over-sized kitchen for anyone at anytime. A two story structure of peeled pine logs, the inn was big, as was everything in it. The kitchen held a massive wood burning stove above which hung cast iron pots and kettles. In the

Maw Kemp's Inn

dining room were photographs and paintings of sled dogs and wild-life. The smoke from the big fireplace billowed up a huge rock and mortar chimney, and people could warm themselves on the stone hearth.

I thought also of the missionary, Luther Schuetze. Luther had trapped and traded with his brother, Ted, before his call to bring the Word of God to the Indians. Luther's church was a rough, simple building. Although he was functionally fluent in the Saulteaux language, he always gave his sermons in English while an interpreter repeated them in the Indian language. What would happen to his ministry if the church burned down?

There were no bulldozers or helicopters in 1938 to support the men on the fireline. The Indians with Wajax hand pumps and mat-tocks were the "brave thin red line" attacking the flames. Cold trickles from the Wajax water bags they carried dribbled down their hot, bare backs, mingling with their sweat from heat and exertion.

A Wajax pump was a heavy canvas water bag with a hand pump attached, and was carried on the back. A label on each bag gave the directions for filling it, and the method of storing during the winter to prevent mildew. A drawing portrayed a husky looking indi-vidual, with a contented look on his face, operating one amid a vast cloud of steam arising from the ground.

None of the Berens River Indians who were issued one of these pumps seemed to be as contented with his lot as the picture depicted. They all knew that the moment a man mounted one on his back, the water would start to seep through, soaking his shirt and filling his moccasins. One firefighter was sure he could have saved himself an extra trip for water if he had just wrung out his clothes and his moccasins on the fire.

Each day, some one brought word on the fire's progress, and many tales came back from the fire line. A man, who had returned to recuperate from inhaling too much smoke, reported the fire no longer presented an unbroken and easily located front. He said it had formed many tongues at various angles to each other.

This jagged front made the fire more difficult to find, and dangerous to the men on the line.

"Six men were lost," he said. "Some of us were sent to find them, but the smoke was too bad. While I was looking for them,I got cut off from the rest of the search crew. Suddenly the fire built up in front of me. There was a lot of smoke; no oxygen left in the air; I couldn't breathe. I ran towards an opening, a natural meadow. There was oxygen there, and I was able to breathe again. I figured those men we were looking for were burned up. But later they walked out unharmed. I had inhaled too much smoke, and had to come home."

The fire suddenly jumped and roared up to the tree tops, according to another witness on the fireline.

"It's something to see," he said. "The flames burn everything on the ground, and creep up to a tree. It sizzles for a time until the pitch melts and catches fire. Then the flames roar and shoot up to the top branches."

From that point, the flames headed in the direction of the settlement, gaining speed and spreading, but still several miles away.

The sun hung in the sky like a mock moon. Shining red through the smoke, it created bright orange reflections that danced and sparkled in the lake. The clouds on the horizon seemed on fire. The moon at night had turned a bright orange.

Luckily there were no human settlements in the path of the flames. However, many wild animals had become trapped and confused. A few of the returning firefighters told of wildlife seeking safety in lakes, sloughs and rivers. One man reported finding the body of a cow moose that had succumbed to the smoke and heat. There, standing beside her was a newborn calf, alive and healthy. The mother must have given birth just before she died. Another Indian, fresh from the fireline, came into the store. He hadn't washed off the grime from the fire, and the soot on his face had lines in it where sweat had rolled down and exposed clean skin. He was Luther's interpreter during Sunday services.

"I sure got a fright out there," he said. "I was alone with a back pump putting out spot fires. When I looked up, I saw a bear right in front of me. He stood up on his back legs, and looked mean. I guess being disturbed by the fire had made him grouchy. I was so scared I froze. Then he dropped to all fours and walked away. I turned and ran, but the bear turned back again, and ran after me. I thought I was finished, but the bear was only bluffing; he came to a stop when I stopped and faced him, and he went the other way. I slowly backed up until I couldn't see him no more. Then I ran."

Those at the settlement realized the fire fighters were losing the battle. The smell of smoke was in the air. The men with their primitive tools couldn't hold the fire, and they returned home, covered in soot, clothes torn and hands blistered. Soon the settlement filled with a smoky haze and the acrid smell of burning trees. Grey ash blanketed the buildings.

Fire brands jumped over to a nearby island on which was situated an independent trader, and I could distinguish staccato popping sounds from that direction. My boss cleared up the mystery when he said, "There goes our competition; that's his ammunition you hear."

Although the people in the settlement didn't panic, they were becoming anxious for their safety. Some of the men took the women and children by boat and canoe to a large rock island, devoid of trees and vegetation. There they erected tents and prepared to stay for as long as necessary.

Soon those who were left could hear the fire. Maw Kemp and

Pearl Calcraft had refused to go with the other women to the island. With the sound of the approaching flames they attempted unsuccessfully to organize a bucket brigade to save their homes. Suddenly the wind changed, and the fire blew back on itself. Men and women alike could scarcely believe their good fortune as they felt drops of rain, followed soon after by a downpour. The people were saved by a miracle, possibly by the prayers of Luther Schuetze.

**

As the weeks went by, my interest in the native people grew, and I picked up a few words of the Saulteaux language. Most of them spoke English, but preferred not to. Thus, I learned that *"Nee-jun sai-ma"* (all Indian words here are spelled phonetically) meant two sticks of the jet black tobacco they shaved into their pipes. *"Kokosh"* was the atrocious salt pork that passed for bacon, and *pak-wae-sakan"* was flour and/or bread. One man greeted me each morning with *"ah-neen neegee"* and what I thought was a mocking smile. I was cool towards him until I learned the smile was amiable, and the words meant "greetings friend."

Two

TRAVELLING TO THE TRAPLINE

I was more tired than I had ever been

One day in the late part of August, five men walked down the Keenora's gangplank and began supervising the unloading of a great deal of freight. The natives greeted them with familiarity. I soon learned these men were trappers who came every year from Winnipeg. The Berens River settlement was merely a jumping off place for them. Their destinations lay three to five week's travel north. *There they stayed, each man alone on his individual trapline. For nine months they had little or no contact with the outside world.* The trappers took rooms in Ma Kemp's inn. I visited them that evening and received a courteous welcome. Later, as I walked back to my quarters, I felt a curious discontent. Their lifestyle was much different from mine – waiting on customers in the store. I reflected on my future with the Hudson's Bay Company. Was I going to get the opportunity this winter to get onto the traplines to buy furs? Now with winter not far off, I looked forward to the company's sending me out to various Indian settlements.

Eventually, winter arrived, the community celebrated Christmas, and soon spring was not far off. Still I stood behind a counter in the Company's store. When the post manager told me I was not likely to be doing anything different for years, I knew I was in the wrong place.

From the start, my aim had been to live in the wilderness. Clearly, the Hudson's Bay Company was not going to answer this yearning. I decided to write to Howard, one of the trappers, at his summer home in Winnipeg, and ask him to take me on as an apprentice. He agreed, and I gave my notice to the Hudson's Bay post manager.

Once again, I experienced the elation I had felt while coming north on the S.S. Keenora. I was overjoyed when Howard stepped off the gangplank of the old ship one day near the end of August. Soon I was helping him prepare to leave for the trapline.

Howard's 180 pounds on a 5-foot 11-inch frame stood him in good stead when he was throwing around 60 pound boxes of tinned butter and 100 pound sacks of flour. He was a quick moving man who walked as if he knew exactly where he was going and what he wanted. I was surprised later in the year that he carefully retained his clipped military moustache in the wilderness. It seemed like an unnecessary adornment on the trapline.

On the 2nd of September, Howard and I set out. Our gear consisted of two canoes together carrying 1600 pounds of freight, so that only the gunwales were above water. A small outboard motor powered the larger craft, a 16 foot freighter with a 40 inch beam. The other was a 12 foot canoe. Two of the Berens River Indians accompanied us to help us over the portages.

Taking my place in the bow of the overly-loaded freight canoe, I imagined what the procession looked like to someone standing on the shoreline.

When we quietly pushed off into the flow of Berens River, I felt a great surge of relief. The two Indian helpers paddling the smaller canoe had no trouble keeping up to the powered boat as it was not geared for speed. Within a couple of hours, we passed canoes going the other direction, laden with bedding and tents. Howard said they were Indians on their way to harvest wild rice near the Berens River settlement. For the rest of the afternoon I gazed contentedly at the passing battlements of rock jutting above the water, and the dappled shadows of the trees above.

Next day, the first portage disturbed my reverie and divulged a few facts of river travel.

As we approached the portage, Howard turned the freighter's bow into the shore near a tall, shining waterfall. After unloading the canoes, he showed me how to tie on a tumpline, a broad leather strap passed across the forehead, the ends lashed to a pack carried high on the back. An enormous load can be transported short distances this way. Howard loaded me up with slightly less than my own weight: a 60 pound box of tinned butter as a base for a 50 pound sack of flour topped by a 10 pound sleeping robe over which was placed the outboard motor. He and the Indian packers carried considerably more. The weight forced my head down so that my chin cut off part of my air intake, and I sounded like a sow rooting in the mud as I tried to get my breath.

This portage contained a muskeg. Step by step, jerking, tugging and wrenching, I overcame the pull of the bog while the load on my forehead forced my chin deeper into my Adam's apple. Each step in the mire released hordes of mosquitoes that regarded us as their personal filling stations. I was too busy getting myself across to notice how the others were handling the muskeg.

Part of the bog was so bad, we had to cut corduroy from nearby Black spruce that we laid down into the mud as a platform to walk on. Although this eventually sank out of sight, it still gave us some support.

At the end of the portage I lowered my load to the ground with great relief. As I slowly raised my head, then turned it from side to side, my neck creaked so loudly in my ears I wondered if the others heard it. Then, with no time to rest, back for another load and another and another. Finally, Howard and I carried the 180 pound canvas freighter while one of the Indians took the smaller canoe across himself.

I was more tired than I had ever been, and my muscles ached. The unexpected pain of my first portage took a little of the romance out of canoe travel. However, I had not a twinge of regret at giving up the soft life with the Hudson's Bay Company. I welcomed the promise of an experience that would toughen me physically and psychologically.

After we re-loaded the canoes, I settled down in the bow, anticipating another half hour or perhaps longer to rest and watch the scenery go by. However, we no sooner pushed off from shore than I was shocked to see another white rapids dead ahead. There had been no way to portage the two rapids at once as they were separated by a high rock wall that made it impossible to cross on land. During our five days on Berens River, we portaged 52 rapids. Sometimes when the portages were a few miles apart, we were able to rest; but too often we came across a series of rapids and waterfalls in plain sight of each other. Often there was no beach to land on, only the rocks partially covered in water. As I jumped out of the canoe to pull the bow up, I sometimes slipped on the wet rock, barking my shins, and even falling into the icy water.

At one portage two Indians by-passed us, each with a 100 pound drum tied onto his tumpline. The men were freighting six drums of gasoline from the Berens River Hudson's Bay post to the Company's post at Little Grand Rapids. As they had a freshly killed deer with them, Howard traded some of our precious potatoes for some of their meat.

I welcomed the evenings after we made camp and had supper. We laid our aching bones beside the campfire, and let the pain slowly melt away. Each night as I jotted down the day's events in my diary, Howard made some disparaging remark about my need to do this. "Put yesterday's events behind you, and look forward to tomorrow," he said. As good as that advice might be in another context, I didn't feel that the logic of it fitted this occasion. For some reason, my writing in a diary seemed to bother Howard; however, this didn't make any difference to our relationship.

As the fire died, the only light came from the stars, and we watched the swing of the constellations in all their brilliance Sometimes we saw a meteor streaming across the sky. In the stillness we could hear the river rushing on its way. High in the sky, a flock of geese passed, calling to each other as they winged their way south.

Later, wrapped in my blankets, I could feel the firmness of the ground under my spruce-bough mattress. This was what I had been looking for. This was as close to the primeval life, I thought, as one could get.

On the third day out we arrived at an Indian village called Little Grand Rapids. Although we didn't intend to spend time there, our hired packers threatened to quit if we didn't lay over for a day. So we languished on the beach while the two Indians visited their friends. The next day we came to the small settlement of Pauingassi. As we approached, a dozen little brown children watched us, then disbursed at top speed in all directions when we touched shore.

That night, while lying in our tent, we heard muted, rhythmic thumps coming from a short distance. Making our way in the dark, through the trees, we came upon two men pounding on a drum. Men and women shuffled, shoulder to shoulder, in a circle around them, keeping time to the beat with a languid sort of sidestep. The unceasing movement and slow rhythm seemed to create a sleepy, euphoric state in the dancers.

I had seen Indians dancing at the Berens River settlement. A fiddle had provided the music, and the dance had been vigorous. At Berens River, only one couple at a time got up. In the centre of the group, as they took their turns, man and woman danced face to face, close but not touching. Their arms hung down at their sides and their faces were completely expressionless. What fascinated me was that their torsos and heads remained almost rigid while their legs energetically jigged like mechanical limbs on a child's wind-up toy. I have since tried to emulate them, but without success.

The next morning, the two Indian packers came to Howard. "We quit," said one. "Go back to Berens River."

"Quit? Why?"

"Wife sick."

"If your wife was sick," said Howard, "why did you leave her in the first place?"

No answer.

Howard continued, "Your trouble is you don't want to work. How do you expect to get back to Berens River?"

"Friend going back. We go with him."

Howard sighed. "All right. But before I pay you off, you better go with me to interpret while I get two men to replace you."

Howard negotiated with a father and son to take the place of the other two. Their names were Abraham and Isaac, a tribute, I thought, to the work of some missionary a couple of generations ago. The physical differences between father and son were so distinct, I looked at them with interest. The father, Abraham, a tiny, wiry man had skin the colour and texture of moose jerky. His nose aquiline, and his face sombre, he reminded me of a bird of prey. Isaac was slim enough that he appeared tall – especially beside his father – but he was shorter than either Howard or me. Unlike his father's face, his was smiling and open. He was friendly while the father was all business. One disadvantage to using these two was that neither of them could speak a word of English.

However, they -especially the father- were far more diligent and active than the previous two. Abraham took my place in the bow of the lead canoe while I was relegated to the bow of the smaller one. My days of lounging while the motor did all the work were gone, and I now had to paddle. At each portage, before the keel of the freighter touched shore, Abraham was halfway packed. The second the canoe touched, he leaped out, pulled up both canoes, finished loading himself, and was gone up the trail on a trot before the rest of us were organized.

THREE

<u>ISAAC</u>

I saw Isaac crouched over a vigorous fire...

After five days on Berens River, not including three stopover days, we advanced into lake country. On the lakes our rests between portages were longer. Sometimes we travelled for an hour or more enjoying the scenery. When we reached a portage, it was inevitably a long one, and joined another lake. Some portages were so lengthy we had to establish a half way point, drop our loads there, and go back for more. Occasionally, instead of portaging, we followed up a creek that joined two lakes. This is called channelling.

I didn't know which was worse, portaging or channelling.

Because of the time of year, the water level in the creeks was low. Soon everyone had to shuck boots and pants, and get out to lighten the loads and let the canoes float higher. Then, knee deep, and sometimes thigh deep in water, we pushed and pulled the heavily loaded canoes up the creek.

It was a miserable experience. The footing underneath consisted of a spongy, sucking kind of mud that floated to the surface and clung like slimy, mucid little animals to our legs. A cold autumn drizzle depleted the last vestige of warmth in our bodies.

As we continued, the days became colder and the rain turned to sleet. No matter how warmly we dressed, sitting in the canoe chilled us to the bone. The nights presented us with a hard frost, and the mornings greeted us with frigid mists.

On the fourth day we crossed the border into Ontario, and travelled on to Deer Lake on which was the store of an independent trader, Oscar Lindokken. As he was a long-standing friend of Howard's, they usually got together for a day or so each autumn. He, his wife and their small son lived in a 2-story log house beside an Indian village. Oscar invited us to sleep in his attic overnight while Abraham and Isaac took the opportunity to visit friends (and perhaps relatives) in the settlement. That night we fell asleep to the sad keening of the Indian sleigh dogs. Tied up all summer, they restlessly waited for the winter snow to release them and their pent-up energy.

Like most free (independent) traders, Oscar had started as a trapper. The day he met Jeannette, who was nursing at a mission in northern Manitoba, he was hooked. He kept coming back to the mission until he brought her as his bride to the trapline.

Jeannette was a pretty, educated woman who, because she married Oscar, spent almost all of her adult life having very little contact with white, English speaking people. When I met them, they had a small son.

(Fifty-five years later, I met Jeannette again. She told me her son and Oscar had become bush pilots and opened an air freighting business. One day their son, who was expected home from a flight to the "outside", never showed up. Days went by before a bush pilot spotted his wrecked plane in a remote area. He had died in the crash. His daughter, married now and with children of her own, lives in Vernon, B.C.. Jeannette, in her early 90's, and now a widow, lives in Red Lake, northern Ontario.)

The next morning Howard and I breakfasted on bear steaks, hash browns, pancakes and coffee. Having company probably was as much a novelty for Jeannette as her big, delicious breakfast was to us.

Oscar sold us some potatoes and carrots from his garden, and sent us on our way with a gift of enough deer meat to do the four of us for several days. Our clothing had dried out and we were renewed men.

Crossing back into Manitoba, we took a northerly course. Howard kept his 12-gauge shotgun by his side, and was occasionally able to bring down some southbound ducks.

On the evening of September 17th, he announced that, next

morning, we were to part. Howard and Abraham were to go in the freighter canoe with most of the freight to drop off winter supplies and grub at the four outcamps along the trapline. Supplying the outcamps now would save us from having to haul traps and heavy boxes of tinned butter and powdered milk later by dog team. As winter was closing in, and the two Indians had to get back to their settlement before freeze-up, there was no time to waste.

Isaac and I were to continue in the smaller canoe to the main cabin to wait for a plane to deposit more freight and the sleigh dogs. "I'm leaving you the map to travel by," Howard said, "Abraham and I will be along in a week or so."

I was looking forward to Isaac's and my being on our own, and I think he was, too. Yet, I was a little uneasy about us, two teenagers unable to speak each other's language, finding our way to a small cabin somewhere on a lonely lake shore.

The next morning, soon after dawn, Isaac and I left Abraham and Howard, and pushing off into the water, headed across the lake. A low, hanging mist surrounded us, and the air was cool and scented. As Howard had the canoe with the motor, Isaac and I were now paddling: Isaac, the experienced canoeist, in the stern, and me in the bow. On reaching the opposite shore, we portaged to another lake, a much larger one, and set off in the canoe again.

The day was warm and soon we were shedding clothing. However, by mid-afternoon a breeze cooled the air. Whitecaps quickly formed, and the lake heaved in grey swells, lifting the canoe's bow and releasing it to crash down before the next attacking wave. Bone chilling water cascaded over the bow, soaking me from head to foot. The first raindrops, large and sparse, warned us of the cloudburst to come, and when it came, the curtain of water almost blinded us. After the deluge spent itself, a heavy drizzle set in and stayed. There was always the fear of a large wave hitting us broadside and capsizing our unstable little canoe; we had to paddle hard to keep the bow heading into the whitecaps.

With apprehension, I watched the canoe take on water from waves splashing over the bow. I knew that time was against us as the little craft could ship only so much water before it capsized. I looked with longing at the shore that didn't seem to get any closer. On and on we paddled, fighting the whitecaps. The rain slanted down like a myriad of tiny knives. Water continued to splash into the canoe, and I became colder and more anxious for our safety. It was impossible for me to become wetter, as I had reached the point of saturation. Isaac, sheltered to some extent in the stern, was a little better off. Finally the keel scraped against sand, and we pulled the canoe up onto the beach with a great sense of relief.

Trying to ignore the piercing arrows of the rain, we raced into the trees to cut tent pegs. Then we unfolded our tent and pushed it up into a cone. After we fastened down everything, I crawled under my robe, prepared to go to sleep without supper as I didn't think lighting a fire in the rain was possible. As I lay there wondering what was keeping Isaac, I heard a crackling, snapping sound like flames in dry wood. Peering out of the tent, I saw Isaac crouched over a hot, vigorous fire, mixing the ingredients of a bannock. I learned that night that a fire-killed pine tree contains resin in its core, and makes good kindling under any conditions. My appreciation for Isaac's skill in the woods and for his cheerfulness in all situations was enhanced.

We finally reached Howard's main camp late the next afternoon. Tying up to a small wharf at a sandy beach, we walked along a picturesque path. Within 15 yards we came to a little log cabin in a Hansel and Gretel type of setting. However, the fairy-tale aura was dispelled by skeletons of fur bearing animals Howard had caught and skinned the previous winter. We walked through the unlocked door into a tiny cabin containing a single room. Against the wall was a bed made of spruce and pine saplings. The stove was a small tin heater, and part way up the stove pipe was a little oven heated by the hot air in the pipe. A washstand in one corner held an enamel basin and pitcher; in another corner was a stack of boards for stretching animal skins. Inside, the cabin emitted the heady fragrance of rodents and conifer branches I have often smelled since in abandoned buildings in the bush.

Howard had asked us to cut some logs with which to build a small log cache or storehouse. The next day, Isaac and I set about falling trees, bucking them into 12 foot logs and peeling them. While we were doing this, we stumbled upon two doghouses made of unpeeled saplings hidden under yard-high buckbrush.

Isaac was a willing worker. He felled the small trees with an axe while I bucked them into appropriate lengths with a crosscut saw we found inside the cabin. While we worked, he and I attempted to teach each other our languages. For example, when I imitated an aeroplane, Isaac said, *"oom-bah-sid-jican"* while I countered with "aeroplane". Similarly, when I barked like a dog, then said "dog", Isaac said, *"anee-mose"*. In a surprisingly short time, we were speaking to each other in short sentences such as, "We eat now".

I attempted to describe a city the size of Winnipeg. The best I could do was, *"Neepawa kitchee waskehagen"* (many large houses). To Isaac, that probably translated into twenty or so log cabins about 600 square feet in size. He would never have believed skyscrapers and city streets even if I could have described them.

I also wracked my brains trying to think of a way to tell Isaac about cars and trains. All sorts of plans went through my head and were discarded. *Toboggans on wheels driven by motors.* The only wheels Isaac had ever seen were on aeroplanes, and I didn't know the word in his language for wheels. The only motors he knew were outboard motors that the Indians bought from the fur traders.

How about aeroplanes that couldn't fly but rolled along on highways? That would be closer to the description of a car. But what's a highway? The only thing remotely resembling a highway in Isaac's experience was a portage.

So I gave up and Isaac worked along in happy ignorance of cars, trains and the like. Probably, during the 60's,70's or 80's, as the people in the north visited civilization, Isaac got to see cars, and might even have been to Winnipeg by now. I would love to have been there when he had his first look.

Despite our language and cultural differences, Isaac and I got along well. We might have become close friends had we had the time. We were about the same age, and each had an interest in learning about the other's culture. Today, I wonder if he is still alive, and what he looks like.

The aeroplane from *Wings*, which was to bring our freight, was eleven days late in arriving. (*Wings Ltd* was a bush flying airline, out of Winnipeg, that hauled freight with old *Junkers*.) As a result, Isaac and I got uncomfortably low in rations. We had started our aeroplane vigil with a little deer meat, white beans, rice and the makings of bannock. However, we soon ran out of meat. As the days wore on, we also ran out of salt, then beans, then baking powder and butter, and got dangerously low in matches. Although this was annoying, it didn't frighten us as we knew the plane would be in soon with supplies, or Howard would be along with some grub. Isaac made a slingshot out of his suspenders, and bagged a few Spruce Hens.

At last the plane arrived. It is difficult to describe the anticipation we felt when we heard the faint hum of its motor far away. I caught sight of it first, and we watched it grow bigger. Finally the pilot set it down gently on the water, then with a great roar of the motor, he taxied up to our small wharf.

The pilot, Isaac and I quickly unloaded a few boxes of tinned butter, which would augment those we had freighted by canoe. We also took from the plane two sacks of flour, a barrel of powdered milk, nails, a 12- foot canoe and two big, bright-looking mongrel dogs that we tied to the two kennels. I gave the pilot a letter to my parents telling them that we expected a plane to touch down at Christmas, so they could send me some mail. Then the aeroplane lumbered out into the lake and swung around to face the wind. With a deafening howl, it was gone.

Abraham and Howard arrived five or six hours later. In the morning, Isaac and his father, after a quick, formal handshake, left in the new 12-foot canoe, which they accepted as payment for their work. We never saw them again.

I have often thought of them. These were men with dignity, content with what each day offered. They gave a good day's work for a day's pay.

On the trapline, which was large enough that a person needed at least five days to get around it, were four outcamps and the main cabin. Three of them were log cabins while one consisted of a wall tent mounted on a bulkhead three logs in height to keep snow from drifting in. It was actually the most spacious of all the cabins. The other three were so small there was room for only a single bed. Whenever we were travelling together, one of us had to sleep on the floor curled around the heater. Howard's "seniority" usually gave him the right to the bed. Occasionally, if I got to the cabin first, I claimed the bed by throwing myself on it. If Howard was in the mood, he attempted to drag me off, and a playful wrestling match followed. Sometimes, if he didn't succeed in throwing me out of the cabin, he allowed me to keep the bed for the night.

In each cabin was one small window covered with cellophane in lieu of glass. As this material quickly turned yellow from the

The author, with a snared lynx

elements, there was barely enough illumination to locate a candle and light it. The "springs" in the bed in each camp were small saplings laid end-to-end, and the "mattress" was spruce boughs. As these beds dried out during the summer, they had to be replaced each fall. They were surprisingly comfortable, especially to someone who had been out slogging on snowshoes all day.

Instead of using sleeping bags as we know them today, each of us lay on a woolen blanket and stretched a robe over himself. These robes, made by the Indians, consisted of stretched but untanned rabbit skins covered by a light duck material. They were warm, but bulky and heavy.

We spent the best part of October travelling to the camps, setting fox snares and mink traps on the way. At each camp we put gill nets in the water to get a supply of winter dog food. I was impressed with the size of fish we took from these nets, especially the muskellunge. We found it to be no small job wrestling one of these large members of the pike family, (a yard long and weighing up to 25 pounds) out of the net into the canoe. Sometimes the fish damaged the net when the big body twisted and

Towser, Fido and the author

writhed trying to get free. As the huge jaws of the fish are lined with teeth, probably capable of splintering a canoe paddle, I made sure I kept my feet out of the way. Other fish we caught were pickerel, whitefish, suckers and perch. At each camp we hung the fish in the trees, ready to feed the dogs through the winter. Of course we ate fish fresh from the nets. *This was closer to my dreams – not standing behind a counter or restocking shelves.*

On return to Main Camp, we set about building a small storehouse on stilts. Earlier, Isaac and I had created a pile of small, peeled logs, and while Howard was building, I went into the forest to get more. I like to think back to that time: the gramophone sitting on a stump sending lively polkas into the woods where I fell, bucked and de-barked trees; and Howard, astride the ascending log walls, cut notches with an axe to receive the end of the next log. After the walls were up and the roof was built, we chinked the cabin with moss that we collected in the forest in our blankets. Then, around the stilts, we nailed tin to keep out the mice. In November, the storehouse was finished and full of our winter supplies. We went around the trapline by canoe, tending snares and traps and building deadfalls and traphouses along the shorelines of the lakes and rivers. The two dogs, Fido and Towser, went with us.

FOUR

AN UNEXPECTED NIGHT OUT

Snow fell during the night, almost covering the dogs and me.

Now, with the winter's preparations completed, Howard and I put all our time, seven days a week, into the business of trapping.

The lakes had been freezing from the shoreline out, creating dangerously soft ice. In the centre, open water made travelling on the lakes particularly hazardous.

Harnessing the dogs to the 12-foot canoe, we walked gingerly out onto the ice, one man on each side ready to grab the canoe's gunwale if the ice should fail us. Just before reaching open water, we put the dogs in the canoe. Then I slid one foot into the bow, and hopped along with the other foot on the ice as Howard pushed the canoe towards the water. When the ice at the edge of the open water was ready to give way under my weight, I got right into the canoe. Howard went through the same performance at the stern until we were afloat.

Approaching ice on the opposite side of the lake, we aimed the canoe at the frozen edge, and paddled as hard as we could, ramming the bow against the ice to break off the thinnest part. Then I put one foot out, gently easing the bow up onto firmer ice until I could get all the way out. The dogs were next. Howard always had to hold Towser back to allow Fido to go first. Otherwise Towser would leap out and wait to catch Fido in midair, and flip him onto his back. This always resulted in a horrendous dog fight, which we disapproved of at the best of times, but particularly on questionable ice over deep water.

After the dogs were out of the canoe, Howard carefully moved into the bow, then got out and helped me pull the canoe onto the ice. When we hooked the dogs to it, each of us took up his position on either side of the canoe, and walked alongside it towards the far shoreline. Once the ice gave out on a lake as we were crossing. On that day, we were headed back to our main camp from an outcamp, each of us holding onto the canoe's gunwale. I didn't hear the ice break or see Howard go under. Suddenly sensing he was no longer with me, I looked over and saw HE HAD DISAPPEARED. Immediately rising from the black mysterious depths like the Old Man of the Sea, he looked at me accusingly as if I had cut the ice from under him. The cold had shut off his voice box, and he opened and closed his mouth like a frog in a vain attempt to say something. Reaching desperately for the canoe, he contacted the gunwale and grasped it in an unbreakable hold. I had no time to be scared; that came later.

Abruptly, I mushed the dogs forward, and grabbing a piece of the dogs' harness, I added my effort to getting Howard out of the water.

He was a big man, and his weight did not easily move out of that hole. I fervently hoped that a great chunk of the treacherous ice didn't give out under this activity and swallow all of us. Inch by inch we dragged him. I was finally rewarded by seeing him sprawled out onto the lake's surface. With his clothes quickly becoming ice, Howard hobbled to shore while I ran to build a huge fire. Thawing out took time, and darkness overtook us long before we reached camp that night.

I spent the last week in November alone on the trapline while Howard stayed at Main Camp to do chores and look for a moose to enhance our larder. By now the lakes and rivers were frozen solid, and we no longer needed the canoe. With the ice hard, thick and smooth, I rode most of the way to Bear Lake Camp on the toboggan that contained my robe and the grub box.

The dogs loped along, easily pulling me on the shiny surface. Fido and Towser were diametrically opposite in their personalities. Towser, the lead dog, was exceptionally intelligent, and responded readily to the commands, "haw, gee, and whoa". But he was lazy, and often let the traces behind him slacken until Fido nipped him in the rump to remind him he was tired of pulling the load by himself. If Howard or I advanced on Towser with a switch to get him to step up the pace, he would stop in his tracks, and turn and wait with lips laid back to the gums in a snarl that said "Try it!" Fido, on the other hand, would cringe at a harsh word. He was always ready to do his share of the work, and always looking for praise.

The day was bright, and a cool breeze ruffled the tree tops. In a trap was the first lynx I had ever seen. I proudly tied it on top of the load, and reached camp just before an early star showed itself.

After tying up the dogs and throwing them half a muskellunge each, I entered the tiny log shelter. Striking a match on my thumbnail, I lit the birch bark fire-starter in the little tin stove. The flames immediately attached themselves to the dry spruce bough kindling, then quickly caught the bigger wood until fire light showed through cracks in the old stove. I put on a pot of clean snow to melt. The little cabin quickly became warm.

At each of our five camps we kept a small amount of powdered milk which we used only for our porridge. The cost of flying in the milk was too high for us to drink as a beverage. However, tonight I thought I would pamper myself with one cupful. (Ironically, at home I hadn't cared for milk and seldom drank any.) One cupful that night changed all that. I had to have a second cup. It was tremendously refreshing, and it filled some kind of a need. After the second cup, I told myself that was enough. But, like an alcoholic, I was driven to have a third cup. Caught up in an uncontrollable urge, I took a fourth cup. Finally, I got hold of myself, and had no more.

From that day I have loved the taste of powdered milk. I hoped that Howard wouldn't notice the drop in the level next time he came to this camp.

When I crawled under my robe that night, I heard the wood in the stove settle down, and somehow the sound was comforting as I contentedly drifted off to sleep.

During the next two days, as I patrolled to Tent Camp and Squirrel Camp, I added two red foxes to the toboggan load. On the fourth morning, the clouds hung low, hiding the tops of the trees, and enveloping the dogs and me in a thin mist. The bleak sky steadily darkened.

By mid-afternoon the first flakes floated lazily down and dissolved on the ice. I noticed a deathlike hush over the land. Then the clouds unbuttoned their underbellies and dumped their loads in a suffocating dense mass, blotting out the lake and forest. Soon, the snow was so deep the dogs were no longer able to pull me, and I was forced to walk ahead of them. Luckily we were close to Fishing Lake Camp, and I was able to find my way in the storm.

All that night the snow fell, and it was still falling in the morning when I got up. Through the one window in the cabin, I looked out onto a world of whiteness. The snow had almost filled the 3-1/2 feet of space between the ground and the bottom of the window sill. An overly-burdened tree branch silently dropped its load of white powder.

With daylight the snowfall became thinner, and about 10 o'clock a gentle stir swayed the trees softly, and I knew the storm was over.

But it left me trapped in the cabin. My snowshoes were of no use in the loose, deep snow. Afraid of another giant snowfall, I decided to leave for Main Camp despite the conditions. Also, I wondered if Howard might worry that I had become lost in the storm.

Within the hour I knew the day was going to be a tough one. Walking was extremely difficult. But far more tiring was my having to continually "break out" the dogs. The toboggan with grub box, heavy sleeping robe and three frozen bodies of foxes and lynx was too heavy a load in the new snow. The dogs kept stopping for a rest, allowing the toboggan to freeze in.

As I was breaking trail in front, usually I was not aware that they had stopped until I looked back and saw them many yards behind. Wearily I returned, kicked loose the toboggan and mushed the dogs on. This happened again and again. I decided not to check any of the snares or traps, but to get to Main Camp as soon as possible. At one o'clock, when I stopped to boil the kettle for a mug of tea, I realized I had gone only about a quarter of the way. Although I was bushed, I decided to continue. By three o'clock, I was so tired I was talking out loud, urging each foot to move one more time. I was in a state of fatigue on a level with severe pain or extensive thirst as I suffered the agony of exhaustion.

Finally I was forced to make camp, something I should have done hours earlier. Unharnessing the dogs, I tied them to trees on the shoreline, then kicked a place for them in the snow as well as a place for me. After making a mug of tea and eating some cold bannock, I wrapped myself in my robe, and went to sleep.

Snow fell during the night, enough to almost cover the dogs and me completely. In the morning I felt great, not even stiff, (the gift of youth.) The dogs looked perky. I ate a chunk of bannock washed down with hot tea, and we set off again. Long before we reached Main Camp, the dogs and I were dead beat again. My walk became a hypnotic, sluggish movement of the legs – a dull rhythm which I maintained by telling my legs to keep moving. My eyes were aware only of the glazed snow one step ahead of my forward moccasin as I continued a mindless plodding, one tormented foot after the other.

Half a mile before the camp, the toboggan froze in again, and this time I left it and the dogs for Howard to get. In the dark I staggered into the cabin just as Howard was sitting down to supper. Too tired to eat, I went right to bed, leaving Howard to feed the dogs their first meal in two days.

The sudden storm had changed Howard's plans. Hunting was out of the question. The snow was not only too deep for him to walk in, it was too deep for the animals he intended to hunt. Nothing moves for a few days after a storm like that.

Luckily for us, rabbits were plentiful that year. Rabbit populations peak and crash every ten years, and if this had been a "crash year" our daily diet might have been low on meat. Big game was scarce, and neither of us was able to bag deer, moose or bear all year. In the fall we did well on ducks and fish. But during December, January and February we lived mainly on rolled oats with powdered milk, rabbits, buttered bannock and tea. I have heard that one cannot live on rabbit meat without some kind of fat as a supplement. Either that is not true, or the little butter we used was enough fat to maintain our health and strength. At each camp we ran a permanent snare line for rabbits. The pads on the feet of these hares act as snowshoes. Thus they are able to hop around easily in the soft deep snow of the bush. There were usually enough rabbits in the snares to keep us going until we got to the next camp. But sometimes we found that an owl had beaten us to it, and left only the bones and a little fur. Once I became lost while picking up rabbits from the snares. I'm one of those people who are born with as much sense of direction as a cement mixer. I can't afford to daydream when I'm in the bush. I have to constantly keep track of where the sun is, the direction the shadows are falling or some landmark. If I don't, I will become lost. On this day, intent on locating each snare, I came across fresh snowshoe tracks. Puzzled, I wondered if Howard was also checking the snares, or if a travelling Indian had passed by. A few minutes elapsed before I realized the tracks were my own, and I had been walking in a circle.

The reader might wonder why we didn't eat the fish we had caught in our nets the previous October, and hung in trees at each camp for the dogs to have during the winter. In the fall, before freeze-up, the fish thawed and froze, and became fly blown. While it was all right for the dogs, we didn't relish eating it. Ice fishing was out of the question. To dig under the snow, and then chop a new hole in the extremely thick ice each evening we arrived at a camp was difficult and time consuming.

We ate only two small meals a day: porridge for breakfast, and rabbits and bannock for supper. [Bannock is essentially flour, grease and baking powder baked in a frying pan.] At noon we "boiled the kettle" on the trail for a mug of tea, but ate nothing with it. During the evenings, the sensuous fragrance of rabbit cooking in a frying pan, added to the delicious aroma of freshly baked bannock, almost made our senses reel. We attacked the food with the same eagerness as wolves with a recently killed deer. We never finished a meal feeling we had eaten all we wanted. Yet this fare was enough to keep us working hard. I actually filled out and gained weight. Furthermore, neither of us had even a cold all year!

The dogs' appetites paralleled ours. Their fish was frozen hard as boards. But that didn't stop the dogs from demolishing half a pike each. Everything went – skin, flesh, bones and guts. Then the dogs licked the ground the fish had lain on until not even a smell was was left. On this diet they worked hard, and remained healthy and lively

As we continually snowshoed around the trapline, we gradually built a hard trail of packed snow on the ice. We couldn't always see the trail, especially after a heavy snow, but we could feel it under us. This firm foundation allowed the dogs to pull their load relatively easily. However, on the shoreline where the new snow had drifted and piled up against the trees, we had to walk back and forth over the drifts until the trail was broken enough for the dogs to get through. Sometimes we saw fox and wolf tracks on the trail where the animals had found walking easier than in the deep snow.

There were times when a booming noise under the ice could be heard some distance away. This sound would swiftly approach us, becoming louder as it came nearer. When it passed under us it was very loud, causing the dogs to jump and attempt to bolt. Then it continued into the distance until it faded to nothing.

I have never discovered whether this was the action of submerged floating ice floes banging into each other and creating a chain reaction, or whether it was a sudden expansion of the ice.

By candlelight in the evenings we skinned our animals, then pulled their skins, glove-like, over stretching boards in order to stretch and preserve them. More often than not, animals were found frozen in the traps, and we took these to Main Camp to thaw out for a few days. Howard usually stayed to do this while I continued to make the rounds.

As the Christmas season drew near, the cold intensified, and Nature brought her own adornment of ice crystals that sparkled like Christmas lights. These were our Christmas decorations, and we needed none other.

On Christmas Day, we stayed at Main Camp with our feet up,listening to the radio and reading. For our big treat we broke out a tin of bully beef, Fat Emma chocolate bars and a bottle of rum we had saved for this occasion. The bully beef, a change from rabbit meat, made this day different from the others. The Fat Emmas, after they had thawed out, tasted like soap. That didn't mar our enjoyment of them, for they, too, were different from the regular fare. The rum we mixed with hot water, and soberly drank it while we read old magazines. Perhaps not a great celebration for some people, but to us, the different food, the rum toddies and the unaccustomed leisure made the day seem like Christmas.

An aeroplane from Wings Ltd. was to touch down at the camp of Gus Wollin, a trapper whose line ran north of ours. Gus' main camp was much larger than any other in that part of the country, and three trappers besides him and ourselves had agreed to meet the plane there at the end of December. This flight was to bring in our mail and a small amount of freight. Accordingly, on 29th December, Howard and I set off for Gus' main camp.

We arrived about noon the next day. All during the trip we had been anticipating some mouth-watering meals of deer or moose steaks. *Surely someone had bagged an animal!* But our expectations were dashed when Gus greeted us with the words, "Welcome to Starvation Camp." However, he had saved two patties of bear meat for us, and I remember savoring mine slowly and with great relish.

Soon the others arrived: Willis, Howard's brother, was 21 years old; Bill, a stocky 30 year old; and Fritz, a grizzled greybeard in his fifties. All of us looked forward with great anticipation to mail from the"outside.

FIVE

HOME AGAIN

I discovered my skin was a mahogany colour

When the Wings Ltd. plane didn't arrive on the scheduled day, Gus reached under his bed and produced a Monopoly game. The six of us played that game for days, taking turns to check the rabbit line, make bannock and cook the rabbits. This was a time of camaraderie. After not seeing other people for a long period, we were so full of high spirits we got more out of that Monopoly game than the game was intended to give. I can recall laughing harder than the occasion warranted when Gus landed on one of Willis' expensive hotel properties, and had to mortgage all his holdings.

One day, we all rushed out as we heard the far-off sound of an approaching plane. But it wasn't ours. The plane carried Cal, the mountie from the Berens River settlement. He had come to investigate a complaint of possible enemy agents sending subversive messages. We had recently declared war with Germany, and people were on edge. Someone flying past had spotted Gus' radio aerial – rabbit snare wire stretched between two high trees that he had stripped of their branches. They looked like two long, bare poles. The informant had suspected espionage.

Cal and the pilot got down from the plane, strapped on snowshoes, and came over to the cabin. Gus invited them in for a cup of tea. "I knew it was you fellows," Cal said, "but I had to act on the complaint. Anyway, I enjoyed the plane ride." They left when they finished their tea, and the Monopoly game continued.

Ten days late, the Wings plane landed. The older men hid the exhilaration we all felt at the arrival of this bearer of news and presents from our families. But Willis and I let it all hang out, and rushed excitedly to the lake, reaching the shoreline before the plane had finished taxiing in. My parents had sent a turkey, expecting immediate delivery... *what a wonderful surprise it would have been*. But, it had gone bad because of the delay, and the pilot had chucked it. However, the letters from home went a long way towards making up for that disappointment.

Howard and I stayed a day longer, then went back to our trapline. We found a good return in our traps, but a few furs had been damaged or completely eaten by scavengers.

As January gave way to February, snowfalls were fewer but the weather grew colder. Even wearing two pairs of mitts didn't keep the cold out, and often we had to shake our hands and bang them together to get the blood flowing quicker. Having to take off our mitts to reset a snare invited frostbite. Our feet also tingled as the cold seeped through moccasins and two pairs of heavy socks. On the severest days trees detonated as loudly as a rifle shot. At other times, sullen winter skies and deeply layered snow created a solemn hush that made one think of the inside of a cathedral. It was a good winter for fur. Every trip around the trapline gave us a profitable yield. Fox, mink, weasel, lynx, beaver, skunk, otter and squirrel – we had them all in our traps and snares at one time or another.

Sometimes a fox would be alive when we got to a snare. Not wanting to damage the fur with a bullet or a bruise from a club, we killed it by leaning on its rib cage until its heart stopped beating.

Slowly, maybe too slowly, I began to wonder if this was right – this torture. I had no compunction about shooting an animal for its meat or for its fur. However, I began to see the suffering afflicted by leghold traps and wire snares. Animals starved to death, froze to death, died of unspeakable terror, chewed their feet off in an agony of desperation.

I pondered this, but kept on trapping.

After the middle of February we got virtually no more snow. As the old snow compacted, the trail became more pronounced and comfortable to walk on. The dogs, finding the pulling of the toboggan easier, moved more quickly than we could. This caused Towser to step on the snowshoe of whoever was walking directly in front of him, tripping him up. The only way to teach him not to do this was to continually switch a willow branch back and forth behind. After receiving a few slaps in the face, Towser stayed back; but when the switching stopped, he was at it again.

As the snow on the lakes began to recede before the relentless rays of the late March sun, our well-packed trail appeared above the snow level. It stood out, a long snake winding along the rivers, creeks and lakes on our route. For a short while this was fine to travel on. However, as the sun's warmth was concentrated on the south side of the trail, it soon developed a sharp decline in that direction. That caused the rear of the toboggan to slide off while the front rode on top behind the dogs. The toboggan was being dragged crosswise. The loose snow beside the trail was now too sticky for the dogs to pull the toboggan on. To keep it from sliding off the trail, Howard or I had to walk along the north side holding a rope attached to the rear of the toboggan. The deep snow stuck to our snowshoes and increased the weight of each foot considerably. The only solution was to carry a stout stick and hit each snowshoe every step or two to knock the snow off. We were working harder than the dogs were.

As March faded into April, the snow on the lakes completely disappeared – but the trail remained. This remnant from winter stood out like a caterpillar on a slice of bread. But now we needed it no more. We could walk on the ice without snowshoes. Unencumbered by the big webs on our feet, we lightly raced around the trapline picking up our winter traps and snares in preparation for a full blitz on the muskrats. Howard's goal was 400 'rats by the end of May.

Normally muskrats are caught in the spring when they are easier to get at and their fur is at its prime. Besides building a main house in the marsh, the muskrat creates smaller houses called "push-ups" nearer their feeding grounds. The entrances are under water, and the muskrat sits on a ledge just above water, but inside the house. To get the animals, we cut the cowl or top off their push-ups like someone taking the top off his morning egg. Then we set the trap inside on the feeding ledge. The muskrats were caught when they came in from underneath to feed.

Eventually the ice disappeared from the rivers and smaller lakes. This was the time to go where the muskrats were, sometimes far from our normal winter route. Using the lighter canoe and no motor, we could portage more easily and move around freely. Taking a tent with us, we camped wherever muskrat houses and push-ups were plentiful. At one spot, a playful flying squirrel kept us awake part of the night. He took delight in swooping down from the top of a nearby tree to land on the yielding slope of our tent. After sliding to the ground, he scampered off to his tree to repeat the fun. Only by running outside in our underwear and yelling at him were we able to make him stop his nocturnal tomfoolery.

I have since learned that it is common practice for flying squirrels to jump onto tents and slide off. One rarely sees this little mammal since it is nocturnal, the only nocturnal animal of its species.

We canoed down creeks and rivers I had never seen before, and pitched our tent beside strange lakes. While there was ice on the larger lakes, we were forced to move the canoe and dogs alternately across the ice into open water and back again onto ice, as we had done the previous fall. It wasn't long before all the lakes were completely open.

Besides building houses and push-ups, the muskrats often construct open air feeding platforms of floating vegetation after the ice goes out. This was a good place to set our traps. We also caught them in their runways, at the foot of river banks, and on floating logs that they sat on to rest. Every evening we had many little *musquash* to skin and stretch. As we trapped out a marsh or a shallow lake frequented by muskrats, we moved on to other grounds.

Once we found a beaver in a trap. Again, I had the feeling that what we were doing was wrong. No one knows how long the beaver had been frantically trying to get away from the log she was attached to – the log that was holding her under the water, drowning her. How often had she struggled to the surface in panic, gasping for breath, poking her nose above the water to gulp air, only to be pulled under again, finally to get relief in death?

Is it right to torture an animal so someone can wear a fur hat?

This was a vibrant time of year. We delighted in the warm sun, canoe travel, longer daylight hours, camping out, (often we didn't bother to put up our tent), hushed sound of fish splashing in the evenings, ducks croaking, geese, a loon. At every new location we strung rabbit snare wire on the trees for an aerial, and listened to the radio as we sat on a rock or log and skinned our catch.

I experienced a wonderful feeling of being in the right place. Although I was beginning to disagree with the use of the leghold trap and wire snare, I felt I could be content in the bush for the rest of my life.

We welcomed a change in diet. Instead of rabbits, our daily fare was now muskrats and gulls' eggs. Many lakes in northern Manitoba contain islands of bare rock, and on these the gulls make their nests. Visiting the islands, we took the eggs from the nests, and put them in a blanket to cushion them in the bottom of the canoe. If a nest contained three eggs, we left it alone, knowing that they would be ready to hatch soon. If there was only one or two in the nest, we took them as we knew they were probably fresh. Besides eating fried and boiled eggs, we had them raw in a shake of powdered milk and lake water flavoured with rum - a wonderful pick-me-up at the end of the day.

The warm weather brought the trapping season to an end. Just before breakup, Wings Ltd. had landed a prearranged plane to pick up our furs, so we had a manageable amount to take back by canoe to Berens River.

Now we concentrated efforts on making preparations to leave. We tied the small canoe onto the storehouse roof at Main Camp for safekeeping, and baled the remainder of our furs. Then we loaded everything we needed into the big canoe. On 25th May we left for city streets, cars and crowds of people. I experienced mixed feelings that day.

The trip to Berens River settlement took only seven days, compared to the three weeks we had travelled in the fall to the trapline. This time the freight was much less, and travelling downstream was easier.

Many rapids we shot gave me the same thrills I had experienced on the midway rides at the Brandon Exhibition when I was younger. As we moved into the current, Howard yelled, "Watch out for rocks," and then, suddenly, the river banks and the trees flew by in a dizzy blur. We both paddled hard, but my main job was to deflect us from hidden boulders. Occasionally we hit one a glancing blow. As I look back, I wonder we never had an accident or lost our furs, considering the waters we ran through on that trip. The dogs, riding in the centre of the canoe, "Hudson's Bay style," took everything in their stride and were not the least excited by white water.

It was a heady experience greeting the Calcrafts, the Schuetzes, Ma Kemp and those natives I had known the previous summer. Some trappers with whom we had played the marathon game of Monopoly at Gus' camp were there ahead of us.

Willis and I took a cabin together on the SS Keenora. The next day, 6th June 1939, when we reached Gimli, none of us wanted to wait for the Keenora to complete the trip to Winnipeg, and we agreed to share a taxi. I have never forgotten that trip on the highway between Gimli and Winnipeg. The smoothness of the ride, the speed and the total lack of human effort gave me a greater thrill than I have received in the thousands of aeroplane miles I have flown since.

At Winnipeg, I visited St. Johns College, my old school, and there I discovered that my skin was a mahogany colour. On the trapline we had not noticed this in each other. Beside my former school mates, my deep tan caused me to stand out like a raven among California gulls.

My parents had driven to Winnipeg to meet me, and they took me to *Moores,* a fashionable Winnipeg restaurant, for the big T-bone steak I had dreamed of demolishing. To my consternation, I had barely begun before I was too full to continue. My stomach had shrunk.

Howard paid me an estimation of my share of the furs before he delivered them to the fur auction. I could afford to take the summer off at my parents' home in Brandon. Then I joined the army. Almost all my old buddies were in uniform.

Since then I have pondered the ethics of trapping. I have come to believe that no one needs a mink coat more than the mink does. I'm not talking about the death of an animal by a hunter or in a slaughterhouse. In fact, I'm not talking about killing at all. I'm talking about suffering: *the terror and unimaginable agony an animal goes through when it is caught in a steel trap or wire snare, and often starves or freezes to death.*

Six

FLIN FLON

"It's a job for a man wearing a big shirt and a small hat"

The war came to a close in 1945.

While I was in uniform I had maintained the vision of the trapline as the stamp of personal freedom and the good life. However, circumstances were now different. During the war I had married. Brought up in a city, Dot was not an experienced woman of the woods, [although I learned through the years that she *was* tough, and could take hardships.] She was willing to follow me to the trapline when I landed back on civie street, but I realized I would be making a mistake to take her 200 canoe miles from civilization.

Also, I was not comfortable about using the leghold trap.

Still, I had to live my life as close to the wilderness as I could get.

Soon after VJ Day, I exchanged my khaki uniform for a pair of black demin pants and a parka, and made plans to get back to the bush.

Flin Flon, Manitoba seemed like a good place to lead to something outdoors, although I didn't know what.

There was no road to the town then, and we had to travel by rail. When we arrived on October 12, we discovered a rustic village. I expect Flin Flon is a modern city today, but in 1945, well… it had no sewer system, for example. A town employee, whom everyone called the Honeyman, came around several times a week to empty everyone's toilets into a truck. Where the contents went from there, I have no idea.

Catching and shipping fish from the lakes north of Flin Flon was an industry that contributed to the town's economy. During the winter, big caterpillar tractors rumbled down the main street pulling trailers full of frozen fish that was loaded into trains and shipped to Winnipeg. Ironically, Flin Flonians had little choice of fish in the local butcher shop.

Soon after our arrival, I was hired by Rod McIsaac, diamond drill contractor. Years later, McIsaac's organization grew into a major diamond drilling company. During my interview with him, he offered me a temporary job packing gasoline to a diamond drill at a remote spot 90 air miles north of Flin Flon. The permanent packer had been injured by a mother bear when his German Shepherd dog had chased her cub. The mother had gone after the dog, and the dog then returned to its master for protection.

"It's a job for a man who wears a big shirt and a small hat," said McIsaac, "You know, a strong back and a weak mind. But if you work out OK, I'll have permanent work for you learning the diamond drill business. Then it will be up to you as to how far you go."

"I'm looking for a job with a future," I replied.

"Like I say, do a good job with this one, and I'll have something more permanent for you."

The next day, after seeing Dot comfortably settled into a rented room in the house of Flin Flon's mayor, George Evans, I boarded a small bush plane to Snow Lake. The plane was so packed with drill parts, drums of gasoline and crates of tinned food there was scarcely room for me to sit. I looked out the small window at the plane's pontoons as they skimmed the surface of the river, and then we lifted into the air.

In a short time we touched down on a beautiful northern lake and taxied to a sandy beach where a man in a cook's apron met us. Marcus was tall, skinny and good natured – just the opposite to what I had expected in professional cooks. He, the pilot and I unloaded the plane, carrying the food cartons to a marquee that contained a large cook stove and two long wooden tables with benches. The fresh, cool air, carried the delicious odours from the cook tent. Nearby was another marquee with sleeping bunks.

"You can use the bunk and the sleeping robe of the guy you're relieving until he gets back," said the cook.

That evening the camp foreman outlined my duties. Each morning I was to pack ten gallons of gasoline two miles inland to the diamond drill. "Know what a tumpline is?" he asked.

"Sure do," I said proudly, "I've used one lots."

"Good, we won't have to break you in then."

In the afternoons I was to fell dry trees, saw them into stove-length pieces, then split them for the cook stove.

The one disadvantage to the job was that Dot was left by herself in Flin Flon. Mike, the foreman, who was a Métis, and a personable type of guy, informed me that it was a mistake to get too attached to your wife. "It makes it harder to leave them when you go to work. Take me," he said, "I see my wife three or four times a year for a few days. That way, she don't take me for granted, and she don't see me enough to get mad at me. So we always get along."

Despite differing with my boss' opinion, I found many advantages to the job. I liked living beside a lake. I enjoyed the woods, the challenges and the hard physical work.

Each morning after Marcus, the cook, helped me sling onto my forehead the tumpline tied to the 100 pound drum of gas, I set out. My predecessor had built a rest station at the halfway mark. From small logs he had made a frame about three feet high on which the gas drum could be lowered while the packer worked the kinks out of his neck. By the time I reached this rest haven, the weight of the gas drum had pushed my head down so my chin was pressed into my Adam's apple, and I was having trouble breathing. After I dumped my load at the drill site and walked back to camp Marcus always rewarded me with a large piece of pie.

That kind of life was bound to lead to a few adventures. The scariest was the day I was helping the crew move the drill to another location. We did this by winching it from tree to tree.

My job, and that of the drillers and their helpers, was to keep feeding logs under the skids upon which the drill sat so that the skids had something to roll on. Then, to ensure the logs stayed in place, we each pressed a foot against them as the drill passed over them. Suddenly, a log rolled over my foot, and the huge drill, weighing tons, continued to move up my leg.

We had just come off a piece of bare rock. Had the accident happened on the rock, I surely would have lost my leg, and perhaps my life.

Luckily we were in muskeg. The operator stopped the winch before the machine either split me in half or buried me in the bog. As I lay there pinned, the others thought my leg was smashed and flattened. However, the muskeg saved me, and I escaped with no injuries.

Another incident that could have been life threatening happened a few days later, when Mike, the foreman was in camp. Spotting a moose in the lake, he threw the canoe into the water, and grabbing a rifle, ordered me into the bow. We paddled close to the moose, and it turned to face us. "That's near enough," I yelled. "You can get him from here."

"I can't risk more than one shot. I don't want to be in the same lake with a wounded moose," Mike said.

"I can almost touch him with my paddle," I shouted, looking back. "Do you want to shove your rifle barrel in his mouth?"

"What're you afraid of? No moose will attack when it's in the water. Get right up to it," Mike ordered.

A moment later, I found myself in the lake. So was the foreman... and the canoe was overturned. Both of us could swim well enough that we got to the canoe and flipped it over.

"What happened?" I asked when we were back in the canoe.

"Didn't you see? You should have been paying attention to what you were doing. That danged moose butted us with its head. You can never trust a wild animal to do what you expect it to. It's a good lesson to learn."

It was an expensive lesson for Mike as his rifle had sunk to the bottom of the lake.

After a few weeks, the man who originally had the job of packer returned, recovered from his bear injuries. I was flown back to Flin Flon and to Dot. We were overjoyed to see each other. People in Flin Flon were friendly, and Dot had been getting to know the neighbours, but she was lonely and missed me, as I missed her.

In a sense, I received a promotion. Rod McIsaac offered me a job as underground drill apprentice in the mine belonging to the Hudson's Bay Mining and Smelting Company.

It didn't look like a promotion to me. I had exchanged the freshness and the beauty of the pristine outdoors for a pitch black hole a half mile underground. We were doing exploratory drilling. This meant the driller and I had to penetrate the farthest reaches of the mine, occasionally entering drifts that were lower than our heights. Always we were in a foot of water. The only lights we had came from the lamps on our helmets. Heavy winter underwear and mackinaw pants couldn't keep out the chill.

We sat for hours in the dark, our feet in cold rubber boots shin deep in the water, interrupted only by the occasional need to draw the rods out of the hole, add an additional one, and reinsert them into the hole. Usually, in the first hour I finished the lunch Dot had made me, leaving me with very little to think about for the remainder of the shift.

There was no safety training or job indoctrination then. A miner, new to the work, had to rely on his common sense and good luck to stay out of danger. One day the driller sent me on an errand that took me into a brightly lit room. As I walked through it, I heard a series of beeps that meant nothing to me. I assumed the beeps were some kind of signal, but I didn't realize they meant *extreme danger, stay away.* When I came out the other end, I was surprised to see two men hunkered down. They looked at me in amazement as an explosion went off where I had just passed by.

Sitting in the dark for eight hours each shift gave me plenty of time to think, Somehow my dream of a wilderness existence had gone awry.

During my military training, I had had the opportunity to visit the Rocky Mountains, and these snow-capped peaks were another vision I carried in my mind.

I talked it over with Dot. "Working underground isn't what I visualised when I left the army. Let's see what those mountains hold for us." She agreed, and after giving McIsaac time to get a replacement, we left for Calgary at the end of March. The first place I visited when we reached the Stampede City was the office of the Crow-Bow Forest Reserve. There I put in an application to become a forest ranger.

The clerk accepted my application without interest, and I could tell he was about to deposit it in a file where it would never again see daylight.

So I decided to approach the top Forestry man in the province.

Dot and I hitchhiked to Edmonton, took a transit bus to the province's administration building, and climbed the stairs to the office of Eric E. Huestis, Director of the Alberta Forest Service. There we were stopped by his secretary.

"What would you like to see him about?" she asked.

"A personal matter."

Not surprisingly, this got us in. No doubt, my reply had piqued Huestis' curiosity. He got up from his desk to shake our hands – a tall, well-built man, pleasant of manner, and seeming to radiate great energy.

When I told him I wanted a job as a ranger, he asked about my outdoor experiences, my service record and whether Dot felt she could stand the isolation and hardships of a ranger's wife. "Have you had any experience with horses?"

"Yes, a little." I answered.

"Good. Handling horses is part of the job," said Huestis.

Then, swinging around in his chair, he pointed to a huge map on the wall behind him.

"There are two positions open. In this northern one, you will be on your own. Mostly you will be maintaining contact with the local Indians, trappers and settlers. Essentially, it is a fire warden and game guardian job."

Then he pointed further south on the map. "This one in Coalspur, 180 miles south west of Edmonton, requires an assistant. You'll learn from the incumbent district ranger about logging, lumbering, range management, game management and other skills you'll need if you want to go higher in the service."

I looked at Dot. Did she really want to live in the bush? She gave me an almost imperceptible nod.

"I'm interested in the second option," I said.

"Your starting salary will be $90 a month," continued Huestis, "and when you get settled in permanently, you will be expected to buy two saddle horses, a saddle and a bridle from your own resources."

This was less than I had been making as a driller's helper, but money was no issue with me. The independent, itinerant bush life that the job of forest ranger offered was a huge attraction.

SEVEN

COALSPUR RANGER STATION

The horse's laid back ears suggested rebellion.

I was ecstatic! Landing a job as an assistant forest ranger, living in the bush, patrolling by horse and snowshoes – just what I was looking for.

After we returned to Calgary for my things, I left for Coalspur. Dot stayed in Calgary with her parents until I called for her a month later. At that time, Dot joined me, bringing furniture purchased with my service gratuities. In Calgary, she had learned we were expecting a baby, the first grandchild on both sides of the family

Coalspur was a CN Railway town of 60 people, one general store, a railway station, a roundhouse, and a ranger station that once had been a Forestry headquarters. The former superintendent's residence was now the district ranger's house. Beside it was a bunkhouse where visiting rangers used to spend the night. That was now home to the assistant ranger.

The district ranger, Al Leaman,[1] was a taciturn, sour man in his mid-thirties. He seemed to think the most important part of his job was to fix the garage door that was falling into disrepair. This struck me as strange because no car, truck or tractor was visible anywhere on the station. After we fixed the door, and painted the garage, we set about building a fence around the entire yard that was perhaps an acre in size. We planted dozens of fence posts, then painted each post white except the top six inches, which we painted green.

---

[1] not his real name

We seemed to fritter away the days, and then the weeks. I asked Al when we would be going on patrol. His answer was, "In good time."

When we finished the fence, and he began talking about fixing up the barn and painting it, I rebelled. "I'm sorry, but I'm going on patrol. May I borrow one of your horses?"

There were fire trails on Al's district that needed brushing out, and a telephone line to Hinton to maintain. He agreed to lend me a horse, and to point me in the direction of one of the Forestry's fire trails.

He led a horse into the corral, and saddled it. The horse's laid-back ears suggested rebellion, and it seemed soured on the human race. I wondered if it was going to give me any trouble.

Fortunately, I could ride. When I was a boy, my parents had bought me a Welsh pony. He was a wild, undisciplined stallion, and used to do his best to unseat me. I gave him the name of Tony after the horse of Tom Mix, the current Hollywood cowboy star at the time. Tony knew he could get a reaction from me by running full gallop with his head down close to the ground. As I had no saddle, I would slide forward until I was sitting as much on his neck as on his back. This put me in fear of sliding down his neck, over his head and onto the ground to be trampled by his hooves. Happily, that never happened.

Another trick of his was to suddenly turn right or left leaving me to hurtle forward in midair. Eventually I learned to control him and stay on his back. Thanks to Tony, I was ready for future dirty tricks that a horse might have in mind.

"His name is Star," said Al, "get in the saddle."

He seemed in a hurry for me to mount the horse. I thought I detected in his voice and in his leer an anticipation of sadistic joy. Moving gently, I slid aboard. Star shivered a little, then shot through the open gate before I indicated to him I was ready for him to move. I stuck with him as the bronc crow-hopped a few times, then broke into a full, unrestrained gallop. Although I couldn't control him, I stayed in the saddle wishing I could dismount as the horse took me places I didn't want to go. Eventually, I got him under control, and we returned at a fast trot.

The next day I set out on Star for the Yellowhead Forestry outcabin. To get there, I rode 20 miles along a winding trail that climbed into a mixed pine and poplar forest, and rimmed a deep, narrow valley. Once I saw a herd of elk feeding far down on the valley floor. These were the first wild elk I had ever seen.

During those still, scented autumn evenings, with Star munching hay in the corral, I sat on the stoop of the little log cabin, and listened to the symphony of the bull elk float across the large pasture. Peel upon peel of whistling calls ended in gusty grunts that echoed through the valley. I had never before heard the whistling, trumpeting and bugling of elk in rut. I stayed out there for several days, patrolling farther down the trail towards Hinton, clearing windfall and mending small bridges and corduroys that crossed creeks and muskegs. *This was unmitigated, glorious solitude.*

Meanwhile, Al continued doing minor renovations to the barn. On my return, I got him away from the barn long enough to teach me to operate the station's patrol speeder. I also told him that Huestis had said I could expect training in the inspection of bush and mill operations.

The mention of Huestis' name might have got him going. One morning we walked the 100 yards to the Forestry's speeder house beside the CNR rail line, and pulled a 2-man speeder onto the tracks. This "iron horse" was a small open-air go-devil. Powered by a gas motor, it coasted along the railway tracks on four flanged wheels. The speeder allowed the ranger to get quickly to strategic places where he could look for smoke from campfires and lightning strikes. Part of the ranger's job was to check that all commercial activities in his district were operating within provincial government regulations. The speeder took him quickly to sawmills and mines located close to the tracks.

That day on speeder patrol with Al was an interesting time of checking sawmills and looking over bush operations. However, I can't say I learned a great deal. He seemed to want to run through as many contacts as he could, and I found it too much to absorb.

The next day, Al had to go to the Edson headquarters. He suggested I take the speeder out for practice while he was away. Riding to the Cadomin Ranger Station, I visited the district ranger, Harold

Parnall.

I discovered that patrolling by rail usually consisted of coming out of one mountain curve only to enter the next.

"Speeders aren't toys," Harold said. He told me about a trapper and a ranger holding a sentimental discussion about old times. When they found they had depleted their bottle of rum, they decided to ride the Forestry speeder to Edson for another bottle. In high spirits, they set the speeder on the tracks and rode the rail to town. When they arrived at Edson, the ranger turned around to speak to his companion, but the trapper wasn't there. Putting the speeder in reverse, the ranger raced back until he found his friend. The trapper was sitting on the right-of-way, unharmed, where he had fallen off. News of the escapade got back to the officials of the railway who lodged a complaint with the Edson forest superintendent. The ranger was severely reprimanded for running a speeder in the dark, and for not checking for oncoming trains.

During the six and a half months I spent on the Coalspur Ranger Station, I often went on speeder patrol alone. I was in a constant state of anxiety trying to do the impossible:- see around the many bends in the mountains. The noise of the speeder's motor prevented me from hearing the clickety-clack of train wheels coming towards me. The first time I experienced a freight train disputing the right-of-way, I suddenly met it with no more than a few yards between us, and a few seconds for me to drag the speeder off the tracks.

I took all the precautions I could to avert a collision with a train. Sometimes I waited for a train to go by, and then followed behind it. That was the most relaxed method of riding a speeder. The one danger in keeping up to the train was in forgetting to slow down at the curves. I knew it was possible for the little speeder to leave the tracks and head off into the bush with disastrous results for the rider.

Harold had advised me to always check with the station agent as to when to expect a passenger or freight along my proposed route. Once he had spent hours filling out forms and reports because he had failed to check the train schedules at the Mercoal railway station before he left for home. "I met a train near the McLeod River bridge," he said. "That locomotive looked mighty big as it came at me. I jumped, leaving the speeder to meet the train head on. Of course, it was a total write-off."

Following Harold's advice, I always checked with Tommy Rose, the Coalspur station agent, about what trains were out there. Tommy's usual reply was, "There won't be a freight or passenger train for another two hours. **But keep an eye out for the work train; it's up there some place.**"

The work train! No one ever seemed to know exactly where it was.

The only reason I never had a head-on collision was the slowness of the trains as they laboriously maneuvered around the almost continual curves of the mountains. Their crawling pace allowed me enough time to jump from the speeder and yank it off the tracks.

Roy Cuff, a wartime buddy who was visiting me, was jolted out of his enjoyment of the scenery while accompanying me on the speeder. Suddenly we were face-to-face with a locomotive. The two of us, as one man, seized the speeder and dragged it off the tracks, and the train went by with the engineer looking down at us.

I felt the time had arrived for me to buy a horse of my own. Riding the speeder to a ranch near the hamlet of Robb, I bought a gentle little mare named Tiny. The rancher and I agreed that he would trail my pony along the railway right-of-way to the ranger station while I rode the speeder back. While riding along, I suddenly found myself looking up at the dreaded work train. The first second was wasted as I stared in shock at the big headlight on the engine. After that, I was too busy to be frightened. I applied the brakes, took hold of the rear of the speeder and yanked it off the tracks – all in a matter of seconds.

Unfortunately, the grade sloped steeply to a deep ditch, and the speeder began to inch down the incline. Desperately I strained and pushed to hold it up on the bank, ignoring the cheery wave of the engineer as the train rolled by. The speeder's weight was too much, and it bested me. Against all my efforts it slowly rolled to the bottom. There I sat waiting for the rancher to turn up with my newly-purchased mare to help me pull the speeder back up to the tracks.

"What," I thought as I waited, *"if this had occurred fifteen miles from home, and there was no rancher coming by with a horse in an*

hour or two?"

Dot had been advised to visit the doctor in Edson once a month. The road to Edson was under construction, and with rail the only way to get there, the train schedule involved an overnight stay.

The freighter, with one passenger car, crept around the hills and mountains at 15 to 25 miles per hour. Supposedly, neophyte engineers received their training on this line. Dot believed it when at times the train unaccountably slowed, then suddenly, with a terrible jerk, picked up speed only to come to a near stop again. Passengers were thrown against their seats and almost into the aisles. Thus Dot jolted and bounced the 50 miles to Edson.

Finally, after the dreary ride, she had to walk several blocks to Edson's only hotel. Four or five loafers perennially adorned the doorway, boldly eyeing every woman who passed by. The whole scenario was dangerous for a woman travelling alone.

There were pleasant days that summer, particularly when our parents visited us. A highway of sorts was completed between Coalspur and Edson in early August. Both Dot's and my parents braved the unpaved, rutted road to visit us and stay a few days. In October 1946, Dot left for Calgary to have the baby. In November, I received a welcome transfer to Lynx Creek, a one-man district in the foothills of southern Alberta.

Eight

LYNX CREEK RANGER STATION

Cam was three weeks old when Dot brought him to our cabin.

I hit the brakes when I was confronted with a logging truck. The driver was in my lane, and he kept on coming. Fortunately, he was going uphill, heavily loaded with logs, and he was crawling. I was transporting my furniture to the Lynx Creek Ranger Station in a 1-ton Forestry truck, and maneuvered past him by swerving into the oncoming lane.

Steep and with many switchbacks, the road was narrow and dangerous. A steady procession of heavily-loaded logging and lumber trucks toiled up the grade on their way to town. Returning empty to their respective logging camps, they hurtled back down.

The road twisted down the mountain like a corkscrew, the right-hand lane hugging the side of the mountain on one curve, and hanging over the outside edge on the next curve. Vehicles going to town (usually loaded trucks) travelled on the inside lane while vehicles returning (usually empty trucks) travelled on the outside lane. This meant that the traveller, whether in a truck or car, or on saddle horse, sometimes moved in the right lane and sometimes in the left lane depending on the direction he was going and what switchback he was on. And may God be with him who forgot which lane he was supposed to be in when he met an empty truck.

So the logging truck I met was in the correct lane at this point, and I was innocently in the wrong.

Driving that road could be a nightmare experience for a newcomer.

Such was the feeling of an inexperienced driver of a lumber truck I was riding to town with later in the month. When we heard the engine brakes of an approaching incoming truck, my driver panicked... he couldn't remember which lane he was to be in. In the frenzy of the moment, I couldn't remember either... right or left? Trying to get away from the speeding vehicle, we ran up the sloping wall of the mountain. The powerful truck took us up until it hung at a terrible angle. Then it flipped over, and lay on its side. Luckily, neither the driver nor I was injured.

The valley in which the ranger station was situated is long, wide, luxuriant, and fringed with hills, the tops of which are bare of trees. This allowed the winds to blow the snow off, and thus provide winter grazing for elk – and for my horses. At the Lynx Creek Ranger Station, I never had to feed my horses in the winter. I merely took them to the hilltops before the snow became too deep for them to walk up there. Then I turned them loose, and checked on them every two or three weeks. When I rounded them up in the spring, they were always in good shape for that time of year.

In the valley and on the hillsides, Blue Douglas fir dominated, and much of the area was free from underbrush. The greater part of this district was game preserve, bordered on the north by Lynx Creek – shallow, fast running, and cold.

Lynx Creek Ranger Station

The ranger station was nestled beside the creek on the edge of an enormous pasture. Comprised of a small log cabin for living quarters, a 3-horse stable and a cache (storehouse), the station was picturesque and a model of rusticity. Logging and lumber trucks had to pass by the ranger station. Fishermen, hunters and picnickers were expected to register. Therefore, I always knew who was on my district.

Although the snow-swept hilltops didn't require my having to make hay for the horses, this location boasted a 9-acre hay field. A team of heavy horses, a hay mower and a rake at the next ranger station south were available to both locations.

The day after I arrived, I walked the seven miles across the hills to that ranger station and borrowed a saddle horse. I had sold Tiny to Leamon.

The next day, Bill Liddel (the assistant ranger from the Coleman Ranger Station that joined my district on the north) appeared on saddle horse, prepared to spend the night. He had ridden through the hills along the 20-mile telephone line connecting the two stations.

During the night, heavy snow began to fall, and didn't stop for four days and nights. When it finally did stop, we found ourselves with more than four feet of snow and very little food.

Nothing moves in four feet of new snow. Snowshoes are useless. Deer can't walk a quarter of a mile. Even wolves and lynx are restricted in the light fluff. No truck passed the cabin for almost a week. Bill and I tried riding to town but got only as far as the pasture gate before our horses were winded. Turning around, we let the horses stagger back to the stable.

A day after the snow stopped coming down, the big snow plough belonging to the Burmis Lumber company came into view. Unable to clear the great mass of snow in an orthodox manner, the operator was forced to push the snow to one side, back up, push it to the other side, move a few feet ahead and do it all again.

Bill and I waited for four hours for the plough to get ahead of us before we started for town on horseback. However, we soon caught up to it, and were forced to follow behind, chafing at the slow pace. Long before we reached the town of Bellevue, darkness had fallen. We still had to ride a few miles along the highway to

Blairmore, and more miles to Coleman. Two exhausted horses and riders arrived at the Coleman Ranger Station in the small hours of the morning.

Two weeks later, back at Lynx Creek, I went to town for groceries. Before Dot had left for Calgary to have the baby, she had told me to send my laundry to her so she could do it in her mother's washing machine. Not having a box to put it in, I cadged from the local florist a box normally used for long-stemmed roses. After jamming in my laundry, I sent the box to Calgary.

Then I visited a garage and service station owned by Buck Rogers, a man with whom I had become friendly. "There's a telegram here for you," said Buck. That is when I learned I had a son. For the rest of the day, I was walking on air. *Dot is OK and we have a son!*

When the laundry arrived in Calgary, Dot's mother took the "flowers" to the hospital. Opening the box, Dot took one glance at the dirty laundry, shut the lid, and said, "Please take them home, Mom. I'll enjoy them more at home than in the hospital." Her roommate in the next bed gave her an odd look.

Cam was three weeks old when Dot brought him to our cabin at Lynx Creek. We handled him with fear and trembling. Neither of us knew anything about raising a baby, and we were a long way from any source of advice. He was a blessing to us, but also a worry. *Would drinking water out of the creek hurt him even though we boil it? Will he be cold at night with no fire in the cabin?*

Lynx Creek Cabin didn't have such a status symbol as a chimney. A stove pipe sticking out of a hole in the roof did the job. We were five miles from our nearest neighbour and had no car to get there in a hurry if we had an emergency. Therefore, we dared not keep a fire in the stove during the night. When Cam's hands showed a bluish tinge in the morning, Dot put mittens on him to sleep in.

As Dot was unable to nurse, Cam's bottle had to be warmed at various times, and one of those times was 1:30 in the morning. Struggling up at midnight to light the wood stove and warm the bottle was a memorable experience.

Should we be strengthening *the baby's formula as he gets older?* Apparently.

Dorothy and Baby Cam

Cam was screaming one day when a logger skied down from his cabin to wait for a truck into town. We asked him in for a cup of coffee. "You're starving that kid," he said. We strengthened the formula, and Cam stopped screaming.

I was religious about keeping the stove pipes clean. Made of cheap material, they were extremely difficult to fit together once I took them apart. One day I was still struggling with them when the time came for the baby to have his bottle. There was nothing to do but light a fire in the snow. If someone had passed by, he would have seen a wild man talking to some stove pipes while nearby, like a native from another era, squatted a woman and her baby beside a small fire in the snow on which a pot of water was heating.

Eventually, I had a pasture full of saddle horses and packhorses. Three were my own. The remainder belonged to miners who were glad to have them boarded for nothing. The Lynx Creek pasture was enormous; in addition, I had more hay than I needed, so I welcomed other people's horses I could freely use as saddle and pack animals.

The main haul road to the logging and lumber camps ran through my pasture. At each end was a gate. Truck drivers were supposed to stop their trucks, open the gates, drive through, then get out and close them. Some of them didn't bother getting out of their trucks a second time, and they left the gates open if they thought no one was looking. Consequently, a good portion of my time was spent hunting for horses, and my work diary (turned in once a month to Head Quarters) showed it.

I had asked the various companies to install Texas gates.[2] As livestock are unable to cross them, I knew that would solve the problem. However, none of the logging companies seemed motivated to do it. Some companies may have thought building gates on Forestry pastures came under the purview of the Forest Service. Finally I received permission from the Calgary office to shut down the haul road until the companies installed the Texas gates.

I wrote a letter to each company telling them that as of 8.00 am on a certain date, I would allow no trucks through the Forestry pasture unless the gates had been installed. On that date, at 8.00 am, I stood at the first gate and watched a line up of five approaching trucks representing four logging companies. Leading the procession was feisty Van Wyk, general manager of the Burmis Lumber Company. Although it galled him to admit defeat, he had had no choice, and had organized the truck cavalcade.

"OK, you win. If you let us through now, I promise you that you'll get your gates before nightfall," he said.

I agreed, and before many hours had passed, a bulldozer and truck loaded with iron rails arrived and installed the gates. The truckers liked the gates, too, because it saved them having to get out to open and close them.

For all our horse transportation, Dot and I had no vehicle that the family could get away in. Dot disliked horseback riding, and it was awkward and dangerous for either of us to ride with a very young baby in our arms.

One day in town, I noticed a buggy sitting near the mine office.

---

[2] a ditch across the road over which rails are laid

I asked the mine manager how much he wanted for it.

"Ten dollars," the manager said.

"I'll give you five."

"Seven-fifty and it's yours," he countered.

So the deal was made. One of my saddle horses was docile and wouldn't balk even if a bear hide was thrown across her back. Although she had never been in harness, I rode her into town carrying a Forestry harness with me, and hooked her up to the buggy. She took to it like a veteran dray horse.

Dot was delighted when I pulled up to our cabin.

One late spring day, we decided to visit Al and Gwen Freeman, the ranger and his wife on the district south of us. By road the distance was 24 miles, but only 7 miles along a pack trail across the hills. Deciding to go the short way, we soon ran into difficulties.

The heavy snow of the previous winter had pulled the poplar trees down, blocking our way. Whenever we reached a downed tree, Dot and the baby got out of the buggy while I urged the mare on. First the front wheels climbed the tree to bounce down on the other side, then the back wheels rolled up and over to slam down onto the ground. Then Dot, the baby and I got back in and continued our ride to the next fallen tree. When a tree was too big to pull the buggy over it, I chopped through it with my axe. By the time we arrived at the Freeman's, it was almost time to turn around and go home, so we stayed overnight and enjoyed their company.

In the northern part of the province where the duties were mostly fire fighting and game patrol, the rangers' districts were enormous. The northern rangers were away from home two to four weeks at a time.

However, the work of a ranger in the south and middle of the province was more varied, because of a greater variety of industry in the foothills, and the districts were much smaller. Lynx Creek was one of the smallest districts, and I got home most nights. Even then, Dot suffered the loneliness of not seeing anyone all day during the winter months except the occasional logger passing through.

On my district were five logging camps and two sawmills. I was responsible for policing these operations to ensure they followed government regulations. For instance, trees were not to be cut too high on the stump, there was to be no wastage, slash was to be piled, and the companies were to keep within their boundaries. Only once did I have to report an operator for cutting over his limits. This young man with a wife and two children owned a small one-man operation. I warned him that his fallers were working beyond the limits of his timber sale, and even took him out with a map and compass and showed him. Still he continued to cut beyond his borders, until he was slapped with a "double stumpage" penalty.

Some tree cutters took their families into the hills, built a cabin and a stable, and spent the winter logging their immediate vicinity. In the spring their employers paid them for their winter's work.

These families lived in even more seclusion than Dot and I did. A prime example of their isolation was the case of two cutters' wives. One lived near the top of a high hill, and the other a few hundred yards down the slope. The women had never met despite the loneliness of the long winter. This was because the snow was so deep and the hillside so steep the women didn't have the stamina to attempt a visit. Whenever I showed up, I was a diversion, and was welcomed like Santa Claus on Christmas Eve.

There were times, however, when I wasn't so welcome. One day when I appeared at the home of a cutter, I found a moose carcass hanging from a tree.

When those people killed an animal, it was to feed their wives and children, and there was no waste. I didn't think the *spirit* of the law was meant to prevent these isolated families from taking the odd animal. So I pretended I didn't see the carcass when I walked by it. As I approached the logger's cabin, the man opened the door and welcomed me with a false enthusiasm, perhaps expecting me to prosecute him for what was hanging in the trees behind his cabin. He and his wife were understandably nervous when I sat down to dinner with them. They didn't have a great deal more on the table than bread, potatoes and meat - lots of meat. I didn't mention the moose. I ate my dinner, thanked the family for the meal, and left soon after.

A logger, whom everyone knew as Doukhobor Mike, lived with his wife and four children on a particularly remote sidehill. Mike was a hard worker and a good provider to his family, but he occasionally needed to let off steam in town.

One day as I was leaving to buy groceries and take my monthly reports in to mail, Mike showed up on skis. As I, too, was looking for a ride, we rode in the same logging truck, and took a hotel room together.

Mike didn't get to bed that night. I didn't know what he did or where he was, but the next morning I located him on the main street. As we were on our way to pick up our groceries, Chief Danny O'Brien, a tall, heavily-built man in the blue uniform of a policeman, approached us. Although he was known by the princely title of "Chief," Danny had no subordinates under him; he was the town's only policeman.

Stopping Mike, he said, "I'll give you fifteen minutes to get out of town, Mike." The fact that the chief knew Mike by his first name was a comment on the logger's previous adventures in town.

We hurriedly picked up our groceries and caught a lumber truck headed back to Lynx Creek. I sat between the driver and Mike who appeared rather morose. Finally he spoke, "Robin, I misbehaved last night, and disgraced you when Danny ran me out of town. I'm no good."

Taking a brand new watch from his wrist, he continued, "I bought this watch for myself, yesterday, but I don't deserve it." Having made that remarkable self-indictment, he opened the truck window and flung the watch into the deep snow. It took the combined efforts of the truck driver, Mike and me to locate it.

Obviously, Mike was a man with little self-control but a well-honed conscience.

Cam playing with his toys at Lynx Creek Ranger Station

NINE

A RANGER'S DUTIES

"This little spring is your sole source of water."

Mike and the others I ran up against in my job – the loggers, the miners and the hunters – were interesting people. However, the job itself held my interest and enthusiasm more than anything else. My duties were so diversified that I could never complain of being bored.

Cattle Range

Local cattle associations ran cows in the forest reserves for a fee, and the rangers were involved with enforcing the regulations. Headquarters notified me by radio when to expect ranchers to arrive with their cattle. The radio also informed me of the number of cows the government allowed each rancher to introduce into the forest reserve.

The cows arrived from each ranch, herded overland by cowhands.

As they milled restlessly around the Forest Reserve gate, the cowhands' job was to push them through quickly. If the cows went through too slowly, some of them would come back out to look for their calves, thereby causing other cows to turn around and go the other way. Amid all the cowboys' shouting, the cows' bawling, dust and apparent confusion I counted each cow as it ran through the gate. Every time I counted fifty cows, I tied a knot in a string.

Government regulations required the stock association to supply a stock rider. His job, among other things, was to put salt blocks high in the hills. This discouraged the cattle from hanging around the creeks alternately licking salt and drinking while trampling the plant life into the soil. The stock rider also moved cattle away from any overly-grazed area. Part of my job was to ensure he carried out the regulations, and I often rode with him to give him a hand.

Judge (he was as sober as a judge) McLaughlin was the stock rider for my district. He rarely laughed, but he did his job beyond what was required of him. For six days, and often seven days, a week he rode, trailing behind him two packhorses loaded with salt. Weather never deterred Judge; spring-swollen rivers never slowed him down. One morning I followed him into a surging stream that I would never have entered on my own. My horse was no more eager to go into the fast running flow than I was, and needed some urging. Reluctantly, the horse stepped in, took a few paces, and then without warning his front legs gave out. He may have stumbled on a hidden rock, or the ground under him may have dropped suddenly. I pitched forward, almost going over my horse's head into the powerful current. The horse fought to regain his footing, tossing his head back and catching me a hard wallop on the nose. I escaped with a nose bleed, but it could have been worse. The horse regained his footing, but only momentarily. For a frightening moment I again felt my horse lose footing, then I realized the animal was swimming. Looking down from the horse's back, I saw the water rushing by.

Sometimes we came across a cow that had stepped into a tin can from a fishermen's camp, and had developed a festered foot. Or we found a critter bloated with gas until it resembled a four-footed dirigible. Range cattle are actually less approachable than elk, and Judge was forced to rope any that needed doctoring. He was expert at snagging a cow's foot with his lariat. Quickly throwing the animal on its side, he did whatever was required to relieve the cow of its discomfort.

Once Judge roped a lean, mean critter and held it while I climbed onto its back. I wanted to experience a little of what a rodeo rider feels, and Judge wasn't about to forgo some first class entertainment by talking me out of it. The cow spun so fast I didn't realize I had become airborne until I crashed into the dirt. That made even Judge crack a smile.

Now and again, a herd of cows drifted over to the ranger station pasture. The 3-wire fence that kept my horses in often proved to be not much of a barrier to them. My horses always recognized the hole the cows made as a way to bigger, if not greener, pastures. Fortunately, they left their tracks and mounds of manure by which I could find them. But, sometimes locating them and rounding them up in the nearby hills meant a day out of my schedule. A 4-wire fence may have stopped the cows, but the Alberta Forest Service in those days didn't have the money to buy another wire for a ranger's pasture fence.

The fall roundup was an exciting event. The ranger district was full of cowhands beating the bush for cows. The ranchers had built a large circular holding corral with poles. Around the circumference of this big paddock, gates opened into it.

Alone or in pairs, men scoured the area, driving the cattle towards the holding compound. I enjoyed temporarily becoming one of them. We rode into the forest and across alpine meadows ferreting out cattle that had gathered singly, in pairs or in small herds. The leaderless cows bolted in every direction, and the cowboys charged through underbrush and under trees at full gallop to head them off. Sometimes, we came to another group of riders with cattle they were driving towards the big corral, and melded the two herds together.

When one or more cowboys arrived with a string of half-wild critters, they herded them into the big corral. Soon cows with various brands milled about in the enclosure. Cowboys inside the corral separated them and put the cows of the same brand into a separated small pen. In this way, the ranchers could collect their own cattle and trail them back home.

A week could go by before the cowboys located every animal.

My job was to count the cows as they left the reserve through a narrow gate. When the roundup was over, I sent in to Forest Headquarters a form accounting for all cows, whether they had been rounded up, were killed by bears or died by poison weed or another cause. Some were never located or accounted for.

Telephone Line
The southern forest reserves' telephone network consisted of a single wire attached to insulators that hung for the most part on trees. This communications link ran across forested valleys, over

hills, and through swamps to join each ranger station and lookout tower. It also was hooked into the provincial telephone system. Before its installation, the Forestry's communication pipeline consisted only of roads and trails. The effectiveness of getting messages from one place to another depended on how quickly a ranger could travel on horseback.

The maintenance of the Forestry line was the responsibility of the rangers. Each ranger had to keep the many miles of telephone trail on his district clear of new growth.

Often, heavy snows, a windfall or the antlers of a passing moose pulled insulators off the trees. Using climbing spurs, I ran up the trees and fastened the insulators back on, after cutting away the debris. Sometimes in old climax forests, the windfall would be too massive for me to saw through with only a swede saw. Then, I cut the wire, pulled it out from under the fallen trees and spliced it. Where the line ran across an alpine meadow,

Maintaining the tree-telephone line

poles took the place of trees. As these poles rotted and came down, I cut new ones from the trees in the forest, and peeled and planted them. When the line crossed a muskeg or swamp that was too deep to accept a pole, I hung the wire on tripods cut from the surrounding bush.

Telephone patrol was hard work. My saddle horse was loaded with a bag of linesman's tools, spare insulators and staples, a coil of no.12 wire for tying on the insulators, climbing spurs, swede saw, axe, rifle and my lunch. Throwing a leg over all this paraphernalia to get into the saddle was an athletic endeavour. I never welcomed the sight of a windfall across the line - a sign that I had to clamber back down over all this freight.

One January in freezing weather, the telephone line between the Lynx Creek and the Coleman Ranger Stations ceased to function. Thinking it was a break in the wire, I set off on snowshoes. I intended to walk the 20 miles along the telephone line to the Coleman Ranger Station, if necessary, to locate the broken wire and fix it. However, the trouble was not a broken line. The deep snow had pulled trees down onto the wire and buried it in many places along the way. I set about the mammoth task of cutting windfall, clawing down through the snow for the wire and nailing the insulators back onto standing trees. There was a mountain of work ahead of me, and I was so engrossed on getting it done that I didn't pay attention to the time. As a result, darkness caught me when I was halfway to Coleman.

I hadn't planned to spend the night out, and I hadn't brought my sleeping bag with me. I couldn't have carried it anyway on top of all the telephone paraphernalia I had to pack. The temperature was typical Alberta January cold, well below freezing. Unable to chop wood in the dark, I fed my fire with small dry branches I broke off the spruce trees. The fire didn't keep me as warm as did the exertion of stumbling around the trees in the dark to locate dry wood. This helped to keep me, if not warm, at least from freezing. Also as my fire kept sinking in the snow, I had to scrape snow away from it using a snowshoe as a shovel. I was active all night.

When I finally arrived at the Coleman Ranger Station, I found one of my big toes had frozen solid. The pain I endured as it thawed gave me a deep resolve to have more respect for below-freezing weather. In time, the entire outer part of the toe came off. Oddly, neither foot had given me any discomfort during the night out, and the frozen toe came as a surprise.

Rangers' telephones were the type people see now on television when watching a show about pioneers of the old west. It hung on the wall, and it had a little crank by which the caller could grind out long and short rings. The person being called, recognizing his particular ring, would answer it. Anyone on the line could pick up his receiver and listen in. Sometimes the telephone was a source of news for all the rangers and their wives who shared the same circuit.

Lookout Tower

People used to mistake the ranger for the towerman who sits in a cabin on the top of a mountain looking for fires. They were not the same person at all. The towerman on my district was Judd Pickup. Judd was reared in the city; his father and brothers were pharmacists. Judd, like me, had always yearned for an outdoor life. He applied for a ranger's job, but as there was none available, he settled for the towerman's position.

Leaving his wife and one small son in Blairmore, he drove to the Lynx Creek Ranger Station. I took his food and gear on two pack-horses to the lookout tower on the mountain top.

On saddle horses, we rode through a trail in the bush, and eventually reached timberline. Then climbing along a rocky, treeless track for hours, we came to where we could see the tower high up on the peak.

A little spring nearby filled a small depression in the rock with clear water.

"Here's where we stop for a while, Judd," I said, climbing down from my horse.

"What for?"

"This little spring is your sole source of water for drinking, bathing in and washing clothes. After I leave, there will be no horse to help you. You will have to tote all your water by yourself." I pointed upwards. "That little cabin way up there is your home for the summer. So be really miserly with your water."

Judd took it in his stride. We filled two 2-gallon canvas water

Taking the lookout man to his cabin on the mountain

bags with a tin cup that we repeatedly dipped into the spring.

The "tower" was really a small cabin perched on the highest peak on the mountain. Guy wires cemented into the rock held it down. Otherwise, the cabin would be in danger of being blown down the precipice. It was a lonely, inhibiting place, made more so by the wind soughing eerily through the guy wires. Judd wanted me to stay for lunch, but I knew my horses would take that monotonous, spooky sound for only a short time before they broke their tethers and went home without me.

Judd stuck with it all summer, and in the fall the Forestry promoted him to assistant ranger. Eventually he left the Forestry to become a cattle rancher near Cochrane, Alberta, and is now retired in Cochrane.

Hay and Wood

The Forestry allowed the rangers ten working days in which to get their hay, and ten working days in which to get their firewood. Lynx Creek Ranger Station boasted a fenced-in hay field about half a mile from the cabin.

Luckily, the first day I set out to cut my hay, Judge, the stock rider, turned up as he always did - unexpectedly. I was in the barn harnessing the Forestry team. "You've got the collar on upside down," he roared. "Well, if that don't beat all. At least you knew what end of the horse to put it on."

I enjoyed sitting on the mower and the rake, driving a team of horses, and later hauling the hay to the barn. There was something peaceful and legendary about making hay the old way. At that location, I had much more hay than I needed because of the bare hilltops on which the horses could graze all winter. However, I put up all the hay I could anyway.

Cutting firewood was less serene than making hay. Chain saws were virtually unknown, and the rangers had to cut their annual four or five cords with crosscut saws and swede saws.

The ranger I had replaced had left only green wood for our fires. I was forced to get out late in the season to get enough dry wood for the winter. This wood was a welcome relief to Dot who had been trying to sterilize the baby's bottles on a reluctant fire of green poplar.

TEN

EX-OFFICIO GAME WARDEN

"You better keep a close watch for that grizzly."

Every ranger was also a game warden. Besides keeping track of hunters and fishermen, we maintained a rough count of the beaver and elk herds. Some districts had traplines on them that the rangers policed. Because most of the Lynx Creek Ranger District was a game preserve where hunting was not allowed, many large herds of elk fearlessly fed on the treeless hilltops. At certain times of the year, Dot and I could sit at breakfast and count up to 75 elk in our pasture.

Often, while snowshoeing silently in the open timber, I came upwind of a herd of elk and counted them at my leisure. I loved the silence of the winter forests, the snow so deep that only the tips of my snowshoes showed. Occasionally a mound of snow on a tree branch lost its grip and fell to the ground, releasing the branch which sprung up as though on its own volition. I enjoyed the solitude of sitting on a windfall to eat my lunch in the muffled stillness.

During hunting season, many hunters arrived to get their share of the elk that had wandered out of the game reserve into the neighboring hills where they were fair game for any hunter who had a license. These early hunters were the lucky ones; they usually got their elk. However, their shots chased the elk back to the game preserve where they were protected by law. The hunters who came later tramped the ridges and searched the valleys in vain.

Sometimes a few elk wandered temporarily out of the game preserve shortly after hunters had passed by. Had the hunters been a little earlier, they would have run into the elk. This happened to a couple of inexperienced youngsters. They had been lucky enough to chance by at the exact time a small herd of elk ventured into where they could be legally shot. The youths had hitched a ride to the ranger station on a logging truck.

"Where are the elk?" they asked.

No one had seen elk for days, and many an experienced hunter had gone home empty-handed. Even I had not found an elk for Dot's and my winter larder. After checking out their hunting licenses, I told them, "Just cross my pasture and head up into those hills. No telling what you might see."

One place is as good as another, I thought. *They'll have a good hike, then come back and flag a logging truck home.*

In a few minutes I heard shots. *Crazy kids! I hope they are not mistaking my horses for elk.*

Just as I was leaving to check on them, they arrived back at the ranger station. "We've got our two elk," they said excitedly. "What do we do with them now?"

Unbelieving, and scared for my horses, I went with them to the kill. Sure enough, they had run into a small herd of elk that must have recently crossed the creek from the game reserve. Through sheer luck, they had arrived at the right place at the right time. Two elk lay dead. The boys hadn't touched them, even to bleed them.

They had scored where the most experienced hunters had failed. Excited but not surprised at their good luck, they had fully expected that when one bought a hunting licence, and entered the area to be hunted, the elk would be there.

*I*n the autumn that I arrived at the Lynx Creek Ranger Station, I shot an elk almost in the same place the boys got theirs. It was a small herd of eight animals. I had picked out a young cow elk, sighted on a spot just back of one of her front legs, and squeezed the trigger. To my astonishment, two elk dropped. One had been standing on a small cornice. As she jumped at the shot, the cornice broke off, throwing the animal onto her back. She had to struggle for several seconds before she got up onto her feet.

On my patrols, I often ran across hunters just after they had killed an animal. In their excitement, some of them had dropped an elk or a moose in a deep draw or another nearly inaccessible place, with no idea how to get the animal out. Then they would ask me to skid their kill out with one of my horses. As I couldn't see an animal wasted, I always complied. But I let the hunters know I didn't approve of where they did their hunting. Most of the experienced hunters used their heads, and thought of all the variables before squeezing the trigger.

Once, while on patrol, I came across a pair who had dropped a moose the previous day. They had dressed out the bull, but because of darkness had decided to leave it where it was until next morning. When they returned, armed with a small chain saw to cut through the bones, they found a grizzly had eaten the nose, torn the carcass and partially covered it with dirt. I arrived just as one of the hunters prepared to dissect the animal. "You better keep a close watch for that grizzly" I suggested. "They're dangerous when they have laid claim to a piece of meat."

In a few minutes, the other hunter said, "Don't get excited, but there she is, and with two cubs."

It was a female, all right, upright on her hind legs, and looking as large as a house. With her were two cubs, each as big as a mature black bear. Here was the classic situation: a bear claiming its moose, and a man also with a strong feeling of proprietorship.' Both men aimed their rifles.

"Don't shoot her," I said. Then I pumped a bullet over the heads of the grizzlies. The sow promptly dropped to all fours and advanced towards us. It was a tense moment.

The hunter with the power saw started it up, and let the motor scream. This caused the mother bear and one cub to turn around and back off. However, the other cub continued its advance. We were afraid the young one would bring the mother back. Not wanting to shoot it, the hunter felled a small tree in front of the cub. The top branches barely missed it, and the young bear stopped in alarm, turned and disappeared in the direction of its mother.

Once I came upwind upon a huge grizzly digging ground squirrels out of their burrows. He didn't see me. While I waited for him to move on, I watched his antics with interest. He sniffed, listened, and began digging, then stopped to sniff and listen again. Eventually he was rewarded with a fat gopher. As he didn't appear ready to move on soon, I quietly surrendered the trail to him, and went back the way I had come. It was getting close to the end of the day, anyway, and time to make camp.

My winter patrols on snowshoes got me into great physical shape. This became obvious whenever I accompanied a hunting party. Inevitably, as they were climbing hills in search of game the hunters were forced to rest while I, feeling no need to take a break, impatiently waited for them to get going again.

Only twice was I forced to prosecute anyone under the Game Act: one a hunter and one a fisherman. These men flouted their contempt for the law, and left me with no choice. I knew both of them, and we remained friends after they were fined.

This says something for the loggers in the bush and the miners in the Crowsnest Pass. I haven't met anyone who, as a group, I have liked better. I got along very well with all of them, and found them a constantly cheerful and big-hearted people.

One day, Bob Sly, bush superintendent for Burmis Lumber Company, asked me to get rid of a persistent bear that wouldn't leave the camp kitchen alone. I rode down there with a number five trap across my thighs, an awkward and heavy tool to carry by saddle horse. On arrival I asked a couple of mill workers to build a trap house.

Trapping a bear is similar to trapping a packrat: a cone-shaped small, log structure, closed in one end, for a bear; a stovepipe plugged in one end for a packrat. The trapper places the bait in the plugged end, and the trap in the open end. Both animals lack fear of humans, and are therefore easy to catch.

While the loggers were building the trap house, I handed my rifle and some ammunition to one of the men along with a lecture.

"Normally, no one but the ranger is allowed a firearm on the game preserve," I told him. "I want to get on home, so I'm trusting you to shoot the bear as soon as it is caught. Under no circumstances, are you to load the rifle until the bear is in the trap."

The worker nodded his assent, and left for the bunkhouse, carrying the rifle. Sly and I continued chatting outside. Suddenly a shot coming from within the bunkhouse interrupted our conversation. To this day, I don't know why that incident happened. More than once the carelessness of people when they handle firearms has amazed me, and I am not surprised at the number of accidental firearm deaths. No one was hurt except the errant logger who had his feelings injured by a dressing-down administered by Bob. He took over the rifle and the job of dispatching the trapped bear that evening.

The field mice were as much a nuisance to Dot and me as the bears were to Burmis' cook. They looked upon Lynx Creek Cabin as theirs, and probably regarded us as unwelcome interlopers. They believed in multi-generational families. That is: father, mother, uncles, aunts, cousins, and grandparents all lived under one roof - our roof. Occasionally, one sat on the kitchen floor, watching us. I remember chasing after one with a shoe in my hand attempting to clobber it as it skittered along the kitchen counter. Sometimes they nosed into our cupboards. One morning, Dot found one wriggling in the strawberry jam, struggling to stay on top of the sticky sweet stuff. The lid had not been put securely enough on the container, and the mouse had knocked it off. Dot dumped the can outside, and the little red rodent streaked off across the snow with an unbelievable story to tell his friends.

We put poison pellets in the corners of the cabin. This got rid of some mice, but they enacted a last revenge by dying in inappropriate places. One mouse, while ascending to mouse heaven, left his body under Dot's pillow while she was asleep. Another mouse gave up the ghost behind the wallboard in the wall of our bedroom. At first we couldn't figure out where the smell was coming from. Dot, who has a bloodhound's sense of smell tracked it down, and I had to tear the wallboard out to get rid of the carcass. We stopped the practice of poison pellets after the child of a fellow ranger died from swallowing one in their cabin.

Packrats created their own kind of harassment. One winter day I went to the cache to get my snowshoes, and found the harness chewed off and taken away. Another time, after I left with a visiting friend on an overnight patrol, a packrat got into a trap I had set for them in the cache. Dave's wife, Mary, and Dot, wanting to put the poor animal out of its misery, shot a few holes in the cache floor with my revolver, attempting to hit it. By sheer dint of numbers, a bullet did hit the little creature and launched him into eternity.

Dot and I have always been interested in wildlife. Sightings of birds and animals of any kind immediately grab our attention. One morning, as I was walking to the barn, I heard a bird song of such exquisite beauty, I set out to search for it.

The beautiful bird music seemed to come from the creek. I soon located a small, short-tailed, white breasted bird on a rock, bobbing up and down as though in deference to some great master. To my astonishment, the bird walked into the cold, white water of Lynx Creek, disappearing from view, but emerging shortly to sit on another rock. Without stopping for a rest, it continued its bob and dip dance.

Later, I learned about the Dipper or Water Ouzel. The only perching birds equipped with oil glands to keep their feathers waterproofed, they are as at home on the bottoms of rivers and creeks as they are on dry ground. They feed on salmon eggs, and the nymphs of mayflies and caddisflies.

The mystery of how the dipper manages to walk on the bottom of fast flowing rivers without being swept downstream was solved after many years of argument. The bird does not cling to the bottom with its claws as claimed, but swims underwater penguin-fashion by using its wings as paddles. Dr. J.W. Jones, Liverpool University, while studying salmon through the glass window of an observation tank submerged in the Welsh Dee, saw dippers searching for salmon eggs. By flapping their wings under the water, the birds maneuvered against the current while feeding.

The dipper is one of the attention-grabbing birds, mammals and reptiles we met during our years in the bush.

ELEVEN

VISITORS

"Find out where the bullet went this time."

Many people came to visit us.

Welcome were the miners from the Pass, sometimes a little raucous, but always with the best of intentions. Welcome also were the loggers.

But some of our guests were pests.

Headquarters had asked me if I were willing to put up two hunters who wished to hunt elk. Apparently they were friends with someone in the Calgary office. As Dot was in the city with Campbell, our son, I was glad for some company, so I agreed.

Although they arrived like true Nimrods, complete with rifles, ammunition and hunting knives, they didn't get around to hunting. They were as well provided with liquor as they were with ammunition, and spent their first evening drowning themselves in their booze. By the time they got up in the morning, it was too late to hunt. On the next morning when I left on patrol, they were still in bed. In the evening when I returned, they were higher than a skyscraper.

On the third day they did start out on a hunt in their car. I had gone on patrol, and returned to hear their great adventure.

"Bill[3] was driving," explained one of them. "When we saw a black bear, Bill stopped the car, and I jumped out and shot at it. Then I jumped back into the car in case it came after me if I wounded it."

---
[3] not his real name

"Where is it now?" I asked.

"I don't know if I hit it. It ran away."

I was furious. "Do you mean we might have a wounded bear in the woods?"

When daylight broke the next morning, I set out to look for the bear, taking the two "hunters" with me. As we couldn't find any blood, I surmised, with great relief, that Bill had missed it.

Years later, in 1964, another ranger, Don Crawford of Hinton, was forced to locate a wounded grizzly through the thoughtlessness of a hunter, and almost lost his life as a result. I know Don well, and he told me the story. The hunter had shot an elk, and when he went to retrieve his trophy, he came upon a grizzly that had taken possession. The bear wasn't about to surrender the prize to such a puny contender as a man. The hunter shot at the bear, and hit it. Now, having every right to attack, the grizzly disarmed the man, and was mauling him when the hunter's two companions arrived and scared the bear away.

Hearing of the incident the next day, Crawford set out with some men to find the wounded animal. With other hunters in the woods, an otherwise peaceful bear was now a hazard to everyone. Separating momentarily from the others, Crawford carefully picked his way over the windfall. Suddenly, without warning, he found himself face-to-face with hundreds of pounds of savage grizzly. The bear attacked. The ranger's yell brought his companions on the run, and they shot it in time to save Crawford's life. He didn't get away unscathed, however, and has scars on his body to always remind him of his close call.

My two visitors from Calgary were in stark contrast to a group of ranchers from Milk River, Alberta. Each fall they arrived fully equipped with horses, farriers' tools, hay and grain, a large cook tent and a smaller tent for sleeping. Keeping their horses in my stable, they quietly saddled them in the dark each morning and were gone before Dot and I had finished breakfast. They hunted every day until dusk. Then they sat around after supper, reliving the day's adventures, exchanging lies, laughing, joking and having a good time. They, too, brought liquor, and I went over each evening to have a nightcap with them. However, there was no drunkenness, and they were in bed early in preparation for a predawn start.

Another pair of questionable visitors knew my parents and through that connection they had asked if they could use our cabin as a hunting headquarters. We gave them our sitting room for their bedroom.

Hanging on the wall was my revolver, and separate, in a leather case, were the bullets for it.

I was on patrol the morning after they arrived when Dot heard a loud report coming from their bedroom. At the time she was in bed with the 'flu, baby Cam in his crib beside her. Simultaneous with the "bang", a hole appeared in the wall just over her head, caused by an errant bullet from my pistol. Luckily she hadn't been sitting up. The men were very apologetic, and explained that one of them had loaded the revolver and fired it by accident. Although I can't see how such a thing is possible, we accepted their apology.

On the next day I arrived home from patrol just in time to catch the pair getting into their car to leave. Before I could enquire about their sudden departure, they shook my hand and were gone. A little bewildered, I unsaddled, fed my horse and walked into the cabin.

Dot called from her bed, "Try to find out where the bullet went this time."

I located it. It had penetrated the visitor's bed, through the comforter, blankets, sheets, and mattress. We never again heard from these two wanabee big game hunters.

A regular and most welcome visitor was Frank Rothenfluh. Frank was 74 years of age when I first met him. I was 25. Our nearest neighbour, he lived five miles from us, separated by a pack trail that ran through the forested hills.

For years Frank and his son, George, had raised beef and trapped on the steep grassy and forested ridges of the foothills.

Then, one day, when George was on a routine fence check, his horse came home riderless. Frank found his son's body in the swollen spring waters of the river, caught by strands of barbed wire. From then on, Frank lived alone. I can't imagine the courage it must have taken him to keep going.

When I met Frank, he was no longer ranching although he still lived on his original homestead. Short, pear-shaped and bowlegged, he sported a big grey moustache and a cowboy hat pushed out to a cone at the top. A natural piquancy of spirit flashed out from his eyes and boomed in his voice.

His years of living alone had not dampened his zest for life, although he was now unable to travel in the four to six feet of snow in the Castle River area. In the winter he hibernated with Blackie and Tippy, his black gelding and mongrel collie.

I was their only visitor during those winter months. Once when I approached his cabin that was almost buried under the snow, I wondered if I would find his frozen body stretched out and guarded by a trapped and half-starved Tippy. But Frank heard my shout, and pushed open the door against the drifting snow, his eyes squinting at the bright, white glare.

"Come in," he said, his voice drowned out by a noisy, yelping Tippy.

I managed a trip to Frank's homestead about four times a winter, and though he never knew when to expect me, his cabin was always clean and tidy. It held a homey smell of burning wood, coming from a cheery fire in his big, old kitchen range. Scenic calendars and photographs from magazines depicting the rural life of many countries, covered a large part of his kitchen walls.

He remembered the sensational train holdup in 1920 at Sentinel near the B.C.-Alberta border by three Russians: Tom Bassoff, George Arkoff and Aubrey Arloff; and how, five days later, they shot it out with the police in a Bellevue cafe, leaving two policemen and Arkoff dead.

During the early years of Frank's life in this area the moonshining "industry" followed on the heels of prohibition, and became a major activity in the B.C.-Alberta mountain country. The hills became a home for many an illicit still. Frank, in his search for fresh meat, or in looking for some of his stray dogies, sometimes came upon a lone horseman with his saddlebags full of bottles. One day he rounded a bend in the trail, and met a caravan of riders and packhorses laden with contraband joyjuice. They were taking the longer but safer route from Fernie, B.C. through the

Flathead range, across the North Kootenay Pass, down into Frank's country, and north to the Crowsnest Pass with its many thirsty customers.

Each spring when the snow had almost left the valley floor, Dot and I looked for Frank, Blackie and Tippy on their first trip of the year. Slowly, for they were all getting along in years, the three friends made their way across our pasture to the cabin. We watched them in the distance as they approached – three small, familiar figures – Frank on Blackie, and Tippy trotting alongside.

Frank was fond of Cam, our baby, and would do anything to hold his interest. He and Dot sometimes clashed over their different theories on raising babies. Interested in how much Cam had grown, Frank would want to wake him, and have a play, which didn't go over well with Dot. Neither did she subscribe to his view that an all-day sucker before breakfast was a pleasure that should not be denied to a 12-month old child. Most of these skirmishes petered out with the loser (usually Frank) gracefully abandoning the field. One day they came to open warfare when Dorothy caught him giving Cam his false teeth to play with.

"You're too fussy," he stormed at her objections, and stomped out of the cabin, not coming in until he was called for dinner.

Many years later, Dot and I, with our thoughts on our old friend, left our car on the dirt road joining Frank's wagon trail, to walk to his cabin that had long been empty. Eventually we broke out of a clump of pine and poplar to enter the small farmyard where I had stood many times calling for Frank to open up.

While Dot was looking around the old barn, I let myself go back in time, and stood where I used to stand, and called "Frank," as I did in bygone years. I tried to imagine him coming to the door. But all that greeted me was a pervading air of loneliness.

Part of the stable roof had begun to collapse. Long grass was growing where there had been paths to the stable and outhouse. The firewood Frank had piled 25 years before was grey and rotting.

Stark and weather-worn was the old snubbing post, holed out by numerous woodpeckers seeking a home. Kicking aside the grass and tangled vetch vines, I found Frank's old anvil, scraps of iron and parts of worn and rusted horseshoes with bent and twisted nails still in them.

We silently walked over to the cabin. A large packrat pressed his nose against the window, interested in what were probably the first humans it had seen. The door was not locked, and we pulled it open. The interior was cold and empty with a strong smell of packrats and the floor littered with droppings. The walls were still papered with pictures, but many of them were hanging loose at the corners or had dropped off. All the calendars indicated August, 1953. That was when Frank's oldest son had taken him to live in Sandpoint, Idaho.

**

In May 1947, a crew of seven recent agrology graduates from the University of Saskatchewan arrived in the area. Their purpose was to conduct a range resource inventory as the initial part of the Eastern Rockies Forest Conservation Board's plan to upgrade the range.

A hundred yards back of the ranger station, the agrologists erected two tents for living quarters and a marquee[4] to serve as a kitchen and mess hall. In charge of the messing was a cook straight from the kitchens of Montreal's nightclubs. He had never lived in a place that was not overrun with people. The only animals he had even the slightest acquaintance with were dogs and cats.

The reaction to the wild animals of the forest by most people from his environment is probably one of curiosity. However, to the cook, it was one of terror. He watched the antics of the scurrying ground squirrels with great mistrust. There was a beaver dam a few yards from his kitchen, and the crew had to convince him that he was not liable to be attacked by a wandering beaver that might enter the marquee. The sheer horror the word *"bear"* produced in the cook prompted the young agrologists to have a little fun by recounting lurid bear stories, mostly created on the spot. However, they quickly saw that the reaction they got was more than they had planned and would certainly result in their being left without a cook if they continued.

One day, the cook made apple pies, and set them on a long wooden

---

[4] a large tent without sides

table to cool. He had worked hard at this job, and was looking forward to the reaction of the boys when they arrived back from their work in the field.

The pies sent out into the forest a lovely, succulent aroma picked up by a passing bear. Bruin followed his nose right into the cook's tent, and immediately tipped over the table, sending all the pies onto the ground. When the cook saw this assault to his morning's work, he didn't consider who had done it. In a red-hot rage, he heaved one frying pan at the bear, hitting it on the head, and with another frying pan in his hand, ran screaming with passion at the offender. Bruin, caught off guard, and completely unnerved, about-turned and scuttled as fast as he could into the forest.

The cook won the battle, but lost the war. When his rage ran out, he collapsed. The agrologists found a blubbering, unmanned wreck when they came back for supper. That night they took him to a hotel in town, and he left for the east the next day.

TWELVE

THE RANGER'S WIFE

The temperature rose to a balmy minus 30 degrees

The work and lives of the wives of the forest rangers were inextricably woven into the pattern of the work and lives of their husbands. The wives played a major role, and they deserve a chapter of their own.

For one thing, they served as radio operators. With the radio room located in the house, it was no problem to turn the volume up and leave the door open. The wife could hear the radio at any time, and relay the message to the ranger or perhaps a neighbouring rancher or logging boss.

The rangers' wives had to deal with the public at the door. Some of the wives even applied the mandatory seals on trappers' beaver pelts and issued fire permits to ranchers and homesteaders who wanted to burn slash. This work, along with intercepting radio messages, was done without pay, and in some of the more busy locations it almost became an all-day job.

For many rangers' wives, life was tough. Some, without help or advice from "the outside," raised their babies and small children in isolated cabins while their husbands were away brushing trail, checking telephone line or cruising timber. Winter was particularly trying because the roads into some of the stations were blocked with snow and the family was cut off from any kind of social activities. A good example of this was the Jumping Pound District. After the last logging operations moved from the district, there was no one to plough the road to the nearest highway; the family was snowed-in all winter.

Many of the women had been raised in cities and a few had come from other countries where the climate was less forbidding. Janet Shankland left the city of Glasgow, Scotland, in 1920 to join her husband, Bill, at the Saunders Ranger Station. Their first home sat alone in the forest, a log cabin a few miles south of a small mining town called Saunders Creek.

One of Shankland's ambitions for his bride was to make a horsewoman of her. He bought her a sidesaddle and taught her to ride. Then, long before she mastered many equestrian techniques, Shankland received word that Superintendent A.G. Smith would be arriving on a visit. Shankland wanted his boss to gain a high opinion of Janet's skill in all things woodsy, including the handling of horses. On the day the superintendent was expected, he sent her off alone to get the mail from Saunders Creek. Helping her onto her horse, he opened the pasture gate and watched her ride away

Shankland visualised Smith looking on when the horse trotted smartly back into the yard, the mail in the saddlebags and Janet sitting straight in the saddle.

Shankland's daughter, Jessie Dean, remembers with a smile the story of her mother's return ride with the mail. "When mother got to Saunders Creek, someone helped her off her horse. Then when it was time to go home, she was given a hand back into the saddle. She rode toward home, proud of her accomplishment and feeling like a competent horsewoman – until she came to the pasture gate and found it closed. The horse, knowing it had a green rider, refused to sidle up to the gate so mother could open it. There was nothing else she could do but get off.

"Remounting was another thing. The horse, whose only thought was to get home, was skittish and refused to stand still. Finally, she tied him to a tree, got on, and with difficulty reached over the horse's head and untied him. Before she could gather the reins in her hand, the horse was off. The picture she presented when she entered the yard at the ranger station was not what Dad had planned. The horse was in a gallop, completely out of control and with one rein dragging on the ground. Mother's hat was askew and she was falling well short of displaying proficiency in the saddle."

In 1924, Ethelwyn Octavia Doble arrived from England to marry Monte Alford, who was ranger at Nordegg. Mrs. Alford kept a diary of some of her experiences while accompanying her husband on patrol. Following is her description of some of her more harrowing times:

July 9th. "Bertie" (pet name for her husband) laid spruce boughs on poles for our bed, and it was comfortable. However, the mice were troublesome, running at the back of my head. They upset me, but when I thought of them as dear little things, I went to sleep, and had a good night.

July 19. Where we camped at the 7000 foot level, it was much colder. I generally have a cup of water by me at night... but when I wanted to drink it, it was frozen.

July 21. We were on the worst trail I have ever seen. I had a touch of sciatica at the time. Bertie had to go first; the trail was so bad and uncertain... down an almost perpendicular descent, across an avalanche of stones of indescribable roughness and uneveness, I made up my mind I would never come out again. I would go back to England, and never leave England again. After about 12 miles of this, it started to rain and hail. Bertie put up the tent while I made a fire and warmed up some deer remains and made cocoa, the hail pelting down on us.

July 22. We had a good night and woke up to a white world. I kissed Bertie, and wished him a happy Christmas. The ground was covered with snow, and it was still snowing heavily.

July 29. We began going over the Sunset Trail. I can only describe it as switchback after switchback, and up and up. We came to a very nasty piece, just a little narrow shelf of loose stone, with a wall of rock high up on our right side, and precipice on our left. Soon we came to a big snowdrift, and our trail was completely obliterated. Bertie walked on, stepping care-

fully as he went, his horse following, and they got safely over. Then I started to cross, walking with one hand on the rock. I got halfway over, and had just called to Bertie when my feet slipped, and I was gone. Down I went, like a rocket, sliding down the snow. It did not hurt me, but I was too alarmed to enjoy it, and went with such velocity that I could not stop myself at the bottom, but rolled over and over. I looked up at Bertie and told him I was not hurt.

(Mrs. Alford had just passed her 52nd birthday at the time.)

For the most part, the early rangers' families got by without plumbing, electricity or central heating. The Forestry cabins often harboured uninvited guests, such as packrats. One day, Mrs. Bert Krause caught a glimpse through a tear in the wallpaper of a garter snake which was moving around between the paper and the log walls. It had slipped in from the outside through a hole in the moss chinking between the logs. From there, it glided into the cabin, and couldn't find its way out. Mrs. Krause hit the wall with the broom to scare it. The snake flopped to the floor and slithered away. For days it reappeared all through the cabin, even in one of the cupboard drawers

Some of the rangers, like Ranger Walt Richardson, were forced to board their children in a nearby town when the children came of school age. Others, like the son of Ranger Dexter Champion, rode miles on their ponies every day to school.

Mrs. Arnold Watt was an enterprising soul. Her husband was stationed in the town of Lac La Biche. Mrs. Watt kept milk cows and sent her children to deliver 12 gallons of milk a day by horse and cart to the town hospital. She received 45 cents a gallon for the milk and 25 cents a quart for cream. She also baked bread, selling it at two loaves for 25 cents; and made cheese and butter, all of which she sold to the townspeople.

When Ranger Harold Parnall was stationed at Edson, his wife taught at Edson's Parkland Composite High school. When her principal asked her to put together a course on forestry, she knew where to go for help. Starting with Harold, she augmented his information through contact with the Northern Alberta Institute of Technology in Edmonton, and by looking up articles in the Department of Lands & Forests' public brochure: *Land, Forest, Wildlife.* The studies included timber cruising, how to apply for timber berths and cut-layout. The students toured North Western Pulp & Power's woodlands to view strip cutting, scarification, tree planting and mechanization of forest operations. They also visited the Erith Tie Company in the Coal Branch.

Mrs. Parnell's course was approved by the Department of Education in Edmonton, and was the only forestry course given at a public school in Alberta at that time.

In 1972, the course was discontinued. It had run for six years, one in the spring and one in the fall, with 30 to 35 boys in each class.

Mrs. Larry Bunbury recalled their first ranger cabin, which was in Drayton Valley. Larry joined the Alberta Forest Service in 1946, and their cabin was so small they had to buy a table that folded up. The only time it was opened was during meals and when Larry had reports to write.

The winter they were moved to Carrot Creek, 30 miles from Edson, the weather was exceptionally cold, the temperature sometimes touching -50 degrees F. Waiting for the first "warm spell" to make their move, they knew they had just a short time to act when the temperature rose to a "balmy" -30 degrees F, and they quickly took advantage of it. "After experiencing 50 degrees below zero, minus 30 degrees feels warm," said Mrs. Bunbury. Luckily, their canned fruit and vegetables made the trip under a tarp in the back of their pickup without freezing.

Mrs. Ed Noble claimed she would never forget a visit she and Ed had from an uninvited guest. In July and August of each year, she always accompanied Ed on his patrols, sleeping under the stars. If it rained, they would put up a tarpaulin. While they were having their supper one evening, she looked up to see a full grown male grizzly bear peering at them while standing on its hind legs.

"I didn't have enough sense to be scared," Mrs. Noble recalled during an interview, "and went up closer to get a good look at it. But Ed fired a couple of shots over its head, and it ambled off." They didn't get much sleep that night, afraid it would return.

The rangers' wives had many experiences they would not have

encountered if they had married city men. For some reason, the public seemed to expect a great deal of these women in many aspects. A case in point is the experience of Ranger Ted Howard's wife one bitterly cold winter night. Ted was the ranger at the Elbow Ranger Station from 1917 to 1937.

A knock came to the door. Standing there was a local Indian, Tom Powderface. "My wife," said Tom quietly, "is going to have a baby. I need your help."

Powderface and his wife lived a few miles away. Unhesitantly, Mary Howard went with him in the horse-drawn shay, under robes to keep out the cold, to where she delivered the baby.

On another occasion, when Ted took his pack boxes apart to make a coffin for a Stoney Indian baby who had died, Mary lined the coffin with one of her own blankets.

When people think of an old-time forest ranger, they might have in mind the romantic picture of the man on horseback. How often do they consider the family toughing it out in a small log cabin?

THIRTEEN

RANGERS' TRAVEL

Some rangers used dogs in harness

Whether on fire patrol, keeping an eye out for poachers, checking on trappers and timber operations, cruising timber or maintaining telephone line and trails, the forest ranger was seldom in one spot for long. He relied chiefly on his horse to carry him around his district. In many cases the ranger had to shoe his own horses, put up hay, and do any veterinarian doctoring he could.

To the public, the ranger and his horse have always been a symbol of forest protection. Together, they have survived hazards and experienced many adventures.

Ranger Rick Radke recalled one of the hazards he faced when he and his horse almost drowned. ":Ed Weideman and I were packing out of Forks Cabin, and had to cross Ram River. This was in the spring, and the Ram was running high. I was in the lead, and began to cross where I thought the ford was.

"However, I was crossing in the wrong place. Within a few feet of the bank, we dropped off into no bottom. Submerged in the water, the horse rolled twice, and I rolled with him. I couldn't swim, and I held onto the saddle horn, seeing light-dark-light-dark with each roll. Finally the horse found his feet, and got us out without injury to either of us."

Ranger Walt Richardson was fortunate in that he was able to bring his wife and young son with him when he was on patrol. Usually out for a month at a time, they trailed four packhorses on which they packed their tepee, sleeping gear, flour, dehydrated potatoes, dried fruit, bacon, grubhoe, axe, saw and rifle. Mrs. Richardson tailed up the outfit, while Walt rode in front. "My wife used to be leery of bears", Richardson explained. "so she would chase our dog up front to scare them off. But I was always afraid the dog would bring an angry bear with her cubs back to us.

"I preferred a tepee to a tent. I could roll it into a little ball, and it was no weight at all. Also, it was roomier than a tent, and we were able to have a fire inside because of the opening in the top that let out the smoke."

Some of the rangers' horses came from wild stock, the descendants of animals that had strayed from farms and ranches and never been caught. There were some good horses among the wild ones, but inbreeding and poor nutrition created many spavined swaybacks. Their life was seldom the carefree, abandoned existence depicted by writers of western paperbacks. Wild horses racing joyfully across open land, manes and tails proudly flowing, were often a figment of a movie producer's imagination. More likely, they were half-starved, pawing into the snow for a mouthful of dry grass.

In 1949, the government authorized a wild horse roundup in the Tay River area, southwest of Rocky Mountain House. Ranger Maurice Vergeage was put in charge of operations. Along with eight other rangers, they chased wild horses for ten days until they had rounded up 37 of them. Those with brands were returned to their owners. The rangers trailed the remaining animals to the Meadows Ranger Station, and applied the Forest Service's brand to the left shoulder of each, then broke them for riding.

Although the saddle horse was their chief method of getting from one place to another, the rangers also relied on team and wagon, canoe, raft, scow, railway, train, car, snowshoes, dog team and pack dog.

One time, Ranger Ted Blefgen's Forestry speeder was able to help two surveyors catch the train they had missed. "Climb onto the speeder, boys," he said, "we'll catch up to the train on the long grade a few miles down the line." When they reached the slow moving train, Blefgen nosed his speeder up to the open platform on the rear passenger car, then reached out and held on to the railing while the surveyors climbed on board. Settling into their seats on the train, they waved goodbye to Blefgen. When the conductor came back to the rear car, he gazed in astonishment at two passengers in what had been an empty coach.

Some of the rangers took advantage of the rivers in their districts to get from point A to point B. Rangers Ed. Noble and Harold Parnall were particularly skilled in the art of making and piloting rafts. Oddly, neither was born in Canada or had the background to prepare them for the type of life they would lead in the Forest Service.

At 20 years of age, Parnall made the implausible transition from a clerk in a ladies' foundation shop on Regent Street in London, England to a trapper in the wilds of Canada in 1910. In 1926, he was taken on as a ranger, and years later promoted to head ranger then to timber inspector.

Noble immigrated from Jamaica in the early 1930's. Life in Canada began as a trapper, prospector and logger. Somehow, he encountered the English immigrant, Parnall. They built a headquarters on the Athabasca River, and each trapped independently from there.

The men learned rafting skills during their trapping days. After both were hired by the Forest Service as rangers, they occasionally used rafts in their patrols, drifting to some point in their districts and then hitching a ride home in the caboose of a freight train.

"Building a raft was hard work," recalled Noble. "We dumped the logs into the river and floated them down to where we intended to make the raft. Then we built a platform on it to keep the supplies up out of the water. Usually the raft itself would get pretty wet."

"One of our rafts held four tons," said Parnall. "On that trip there was Ed Noble, Nick Lingle, Mrs. Lingle, me and all our supplies. The Lingles were headed for their trapline and their supplies were for six months. One of us stood at each end to steer it with long poles we called sweeps."

Noble remembered hitting lots of white water on their trips, but the rafts broke the water and rode well. "You had to know the river and stay in the current. If you got off to one side and bumped on a rock, it swept the raft around and you were in trouble."

One time, two trappers, Charlie White and Bob Harwood, passed on their raft close to Noble's and Parnall's cabin. Shortly after, they found themselves stuck on some rocks . White stayed on board while Noble, Parnall, Harwood and two other men pried the raft free. After they got it afloat, Harwood, afraid it would take off downstream without him, jumped into the swift current to catch it. But the raft was too fast for him, and Harwood stumbled and vanished into the water before the eyes of the others, his hat, bobbing and twirling on the current and finally disappearing around a bend in the river. He was never seen again, although White, Noble and Parnall spent days searching for his body.

In the winter the rivers presented a different element of risk for the rangers. Before the advent of the snowmobile, snowshoes and dogs were often the only method of travel.

Ranger Charlie Chapman remembered dropping through the ice in the Smoky River while wearing snowshoes. "I was using the *squaw hitch* for harness," Chapman said. "This is usually made from fish net sideline and is fashioned so a person can put his snowshoes on or take them off just by twisting his feet a certain way."

According to Chapman, if he had been wearing any other kind of harness, he would never have been able to save himself. "I had a little Hudson Bay axe which I drove into the ice. This held me momentarily from going under, and I was able to slowly drag myself up. The minute I got out, my clothes stiffened in the cold. I quickly built a fire and thawed out."

Some rangers used dogs in harness. Others preferred to pack their supplies on their dogs' backs. Harold Parnall looked back on those days with some nostalgia.

"When I was stationed at Lovett," Parnall reflected, "I

packed my mail each week from the post office in Foothills on a big 170-pound dog by the name of Phirpo. But when I went to Edson for grub, about a 70-mile round trip, I'd use the toboggan with the dogs in harness. I loaded about 75 pounds per dog."

Ranger John Sutter's mode of travel was mainly by outboard motor boat in summer and dog team in winter. Patrolling the Athabasca River, his usual beat was between Embarras Portage and Fort Chipewyan, his headquarters. At times in the winter, Sutter experienced blizzards on Lake Athabasca. Stopping and stretching out his sleeping bag in the carryall (sled), he crawled in to wait out the storm while his dogs curled up in the snow.

Sutter took possession of a lifeboat from one of the old sternwheelers. After installing a single cylinder, 2-cycle engine with a long stroke, he felt he had a boat he could take on all kinds of rough water. But the motor made the boat vibrate so badly that Sutter had to stand up and let his knees go slack whenever he wanted to make out something specific on shore. He sat in the stern, smoking his pipe, a puff of smoke seeming to belch out each time the engine fired.

Mostly, the rangers travelled on foot, by water or by horse. But a few owned vehicles. Gordon Watt, stationed at Entrance, had an old truck which, through necessity, became the local ambulance.

"Sometimes after working all day," Watt remembered, "I'd have to take a hospital case into Edson, a round trip of 135 miles. One night I made the trip twice, getting home at five in the morning, I had driven a local girl to the hospital with a broken leg after her horse had thrown her. When I got home, I found my daughter had broken her leg while I was away. So I set off again for Edson."

Watt's truck went on several other interesting missions of mercy. "I remember when I lost a race with the stork. The wife of my assistant, Alec Haight, was going to have a baby. I took my wife along with me and we set off to Edson as fast as we could. It was snowing heavily and the road was so bad I had to stop to put the chains on. At Obed, the baby began to come. We turned in at Bob Maguire's house and I ran in, shouting: 'Put the kettle on.' Mrs. Maguire and my wife looked after things; the baby was born and Hazel never even got a cold out of it. The Lord was with us that night. Another time I took a lady to Jasper, and her baby was born on the hospital steps.

"One night," continued Watt, "four boys were overcome in their panel truck by carbon monoxide. One of them had awakened and made his way to the ranger station. Taking a couple of men with me, we jumped in the car and hurried to them. The three were unconscious. We put them in my car and raced to Jasper. The men splashed cold water on the boys' faces all the way to keep them awake. Two of them stayed in the hospital for three months."

Ed Noble, when he was promoted to timber inspector, had one of the few trucks in the Edson area. He had never owned nor driven an automobile. When he was issued a truck by the Forest Service, he had to pick it up in Edmonton. "It was in a garage, and I wasn't skillful enough to back it out," Noble recollected. "so I told the mechanic to bring it out and gas it up. Then I got in and very carefully began to drive home. Rather than go on the main thoroughfares of Edmonton, I took the secondary streets, stopping at every corner to look in both directions. Somehow or other, I got outside the city and onto the highway. On the way home, I got stuck twice. One of these times a fellow passed with a team of horses and I asked him to give me a pull out of the mud. He looked at me and said, 'I wouldn't pull that machine out of there if it had to stay forever.' I guess he didn't like cars."

Although superintendents didn't have to travel as much as their men, their trips around the forests were fraught with as many difficulties. Eric Huestis recalled travelling, when he was a superintendent, from his headquarters at Coalspur, in the Coal Branch, to Entrance, a few miles north and west of Hinton. First, he had to catch the train to Edson and stay overnight. The next morning, he took a train to Entrance. After finishing his work, he used up the better part of another two days to get home. Today the trip takes 45 minutes.

Another old-time mode of travel was aerial cable. In the days when ferries were few and bridges were fewer, people got themselves and their belongings across the larger rivers by a gondola rigged on a hand-operated cable pulley. One used for years by the Forestry, and by other local people, was erected across the Saskatchewan River near Rocky Mountain House by the Dominion Irrigation Department. Pieces of the cable, which carried a gondola across the Athabasca River near Entrance, are still visible.

The rangers used a variety of methods to get around their districts, but only once in the history of the Forest Service did a ranger use a bicycle.

Tom F. was a married man with six children. Not only was he not accustomed to horses, he wanted nothing to do with them. When he was hired to man the Rimbey Ranger Station, he attempted to get around his district on foot. However, his supervisors, Timber Inspector Ray Smuland and Director of Forestry Eric Huestis, put pressure on him to get transportation. Finally, in desperation, Tom bought a bicycle and bounced along on two wheels over the bush roads and trails with his working tools tied onto a carrier on the back.

Huestis' reaction when he heard about the bicycle was exemplified by his letter to Smuland which contained the sentence: "I fail to see why you haven't insisted that this man have proper transportation long before now."

Tom still wanted nothing to do with horses. However, under pressure, he bought a 1929 Ford. On the third time out, way back in the bush, the car wouldn't start. Tom cranked away at the front of it until he cranked himself into a temper. Stepping back, he wearily raised his right arm and hurled the crank through the windshield. Then he walked home and went back to his bicycle, which he insisted using until he left the Forest Service.

From 1888 to the end of the 1940's, the rangers' methods of travel changed very little. True, speeders and trucks had appeared, but the saddlehorse was still the chief means of transportation. From the early 1950's, however, the methods by which rangers got around their districts and got to fires was to change dramatically. The introduction of 4WD trucks and helicopters was beyond what men like Ed Noble, Dexter Champion and John Sutter could have imagined during the quiet 1930's.

FOURTEEN

RANGERS AND BEARS

The bear hooked its claws into Lyle's foot

Two occasional acquaintances of the rangers were the black bear and the grizzly. While the bears and rangers shared their environment peacefully enough, there was an occasional altercation, which the man usually lost. One of the most dramatic examples in ranger history was the experience of Ranger Ron Lyle.

Lyle, a lean, quiet-spoken man, suffered for many years from an argument he had with a black bear. On August 7, 1952, he was searching for his horse through the woods south of Rough Creek near Rocky Mountain House. He had left the Meadows Ranger Cabin early that morning with a bridle and a tin full of oats. A fine drizzle added to the flood of the nearby Ram River and made travel through the wet bush downright uncomfortable.

After searching and calling, Lyle heard the bell one of the horses carried around its neck. The sound came from the depths of a deep draw. Beating his way through the tangled underbrush, he stopped now and then to catch the sound of the bell. During one of these pauses he heard a growl and, turning his head, he saw above the willows and alders the glossy back of a black bear advancing towards him. Lyle was unarmed. His decision to run was automatic. With the bear in hot pursuit, Ron reached a tree about 20 inches in diameter, and began shinnying up the trunk faster than he had ever climbed before. He was six feet up when the bear reached the tree and swiped at Lyle's foot, sinking its claws through the heel of his rubber boot which came off and fell to the ground.

Determined to save himself, Lyle continued climbing until he reached the top and settled himself into a crotch of the tree.

The bear came up after him. When it reached Lyle, it took another swipe at his boot but missed. The momentum of the swing dislodged the animal and it lost its balance. With a great feeling of relief, Lyle watched the bear fall. Then to his dismay he saw the bear twist with amazing agility near the ground and break its fall by digging all four claws into the tree's trunk. To this day, Lyle remains awed at the strength displayed by the bear at that moment.

Now Bruin was angry. Quickly and single-mindedly, it went back up the tree. With greater accuracy this time, the bear hooked its claws into Lyle's foot, pulled him out of his position in the crotch of the tree and sent him somersaulting 30 feet to the ground.

To Lyle, his fall seemed slow, almost leisurely. As he turned over in the air, he could see the bear looking down from high up in the tree. Lyle admitted he felt strangely relaxed and accepted what he considered inevitable death. He never felt the impact with the ground.

When Ron awoke later, he found the bear had dragged him under the long limbs of a large spruce tree, presumably to return for a meal at a later time. Staggering to his feet, Lyle stumbled numbly off in the direction of the Meadows Cabin. He hadn't gone 30 yards before he found his horses. Luckily, the belled horse allowed itself to be caught, and removing the belt from his trousers, Lyle looped it through the bell strap on the mare's neck. He was too weak to get on the horse's back, and he hobbled alongside her, pulled and supported by the big animal. The mare wanted to follow the others and only through continual urging could Lyle get her to walk home, half dragging the human ballast after her. Full of pain, Lyle staggered along the uneven terrain up a sidehill and through a creek.

At the Meadows cabin, Ranger Ed Wiedeman saw the man and horse coming across the pasture. When he learned what had happened, he telephoned Ranger Ben Shantz at Shunda, who relayed the message 35 miles to Rocky Mountain House Forest Service Headquarters.

The rescue of Ron Lyle from the Meadows Cabin involved considerable difficulty. Ranger Don McDonald and Doctor Greenway, both of Rocky Mountain House, found the ferry across the North Saskatchewan River at Saunders not operating, and had to cross on a cable car high across the boiling rapids. The car consisted of two planks bracketed to a pair of pulley wheels that took the cable across the river. Progress was obtained through a lever in the basket that gripped the cable and had to be jerked back and forth by one of the men in order to propel them forward. Once across, they were met by Weideman on a tractor. On the way to the cabin, the tractor became mired on the water soaked trail, and the men had to walk the remaining seven miles. They arrived at 2 o'clock in the morning.

The doctor could see that Lyle should be moved only by aircraft. A Beaver aeroplane was dispatched, but the pilot refused to land on the small water soaked field and flew back home. Finally, someone remembered Mel Cipperley, an automobile dealer in Olds. Cipperley was known for his bush flying skills and iron nerve. Picking up Ranger Harry Edgecombe, Cipperley headed for Meadows Cabin in his Aeronca Super Chief aircraft.

After landing, the pilot saw he would be unable to take off until some work was done on the field to create a temporary runway. On the evening of the next day, with Lyle strapped into the plane, Cipperley took off with barely enough clearance. Arriving at Rocky Mountain House in the dark he found the townspeople in their cars had ringed the landing field with headlights. After a great deal of difficulty, Ron was transferred to an ambulance and hospitalised with a crushed vertebra.

Lyle's attitude toward bears remained positive. He said, "I've had people ask me if I hate bears since my ordeal. I don't. They are a part of our wildlife, and a bear to me is a pretty animal to see. But you've got to have respect for them. I still think bears should be part of our environment and should be protected."

In the mind of the bear that had injured Lyle, the attack had been provoked. Investigation later showed that he had inadvertently interrupted the bear when it had been enjoying a meal of elk meat.

"I still like to watch bears," said Lyle during an interview. "One summer, at the Meadows Cabin, a 2-year old bear used to come every morning to see what I had left in the garbage pit. He stayed with me all summer. Never once did he come to my door; he never tried to enter my cabin. He would pick up the scraps from the pit, then run into the pines, and I wouldn't see him until the next morning. I really liked that bear, and I wouldn't have harmed him for anything."

During the late 1940s, Ranger Jud Pickup used to patrol to a line cabin at the edge of the Kananaskis and Spray Lakes Districts. He found it easier to keep some staples, such as flour, in the cabin rather than pack them around with him. After checking the treeline telephone, he would stay overnight in the cabin, and leave for home the next day.

Twice, in Jud's absence, a bear got in and scattered the flour and other grub all over the cabin. Jud tried a lock on the door, but the bears knocked the door off its hinges. Then he tied the food so high the bears couldn't reach it; but the bears came through the roof and got it.

Calgary Power had built a cabin a half a mile farther on. They told Jud they had a bear-proof cabin, with bars on the windows and door, and he could use it any time he found his place ransacked. One day he got to the Calgary Power cabin just after dusk. From a distance, everything looked all right – the door was still in its place, and the windows looked OK. But when he got closer, he saw that the bear had gone through the wall. Cans of paint had tooth marks through them about the size of a .303 bullet. There was paint all over the ceiling and the walls. All the food the bear had taken a liking to was eaten; what it didn't like, it spread all around the cabin. Jud was knee deep in junk.

Ranger Joe Passamara lost the temporary use of a perfectly good broom when he found a bear in one of his outcabins. As Joe approached, the bear panicked and ran out the open door. Joe broke the broom handle across the bear's rear end as it passed him. Some bears will attack without apparent provocation. Ranger Bob Diesel and his assistant became painfully aware of that fact while staying at a Forestry outcabin at the confluence of the Athabasca and Lac La Biche Rivers. On reaching the cabin, they pulled their canoe onto the bank, turned it upside down, and went inside to stay for the night. At daybreak, they were rudely awakened by a black bear attempting to come through the window. The commotion the two men made discouraged the bear, and he backed out.

The rangers, widely awake by this time, decided to stay up. The assistant went to the river for a pail of water to make a pot of porridge, and discovered the bear had ripped an 18-inch hole in the canoe. Many a trapper has learned, as the two rangers did, that an upturned canoe or boat inevitably excites a bear's curiosity.

Activities were curtailed for the day while Diesel fixed the rip by gluing heavy canvas from his bedroll over tin from a can with which he had covered the hole.

Meanwhile the bear was still in the vicinity. Diesel looked up from his efforts on the canoe when he heard his assistant shouting. The assistant was on one side of a large windfall, and the bear on the other side attempting to get at him.

Diesel stood up and shouted at the bear. Bruin, noting an easier target with no windfall to impede him, left the assistant, and rushed up the bank straight for Diesel. Happily, the ranger was wearing a pistol. He emptied the full magazine into the bear, and it wasn't until it had absorbed the sixth round that it finally rolled, only about ten feet from where Diesel stood.

Another unprovoked attack occurred on the long weekend of September 4, 1959. A carload of fishermen set out from Edmonton to fish at Antler Creek, north of Cadomin. The next morning, they dropped off one of their companions, Lyndon Hooper, who intended to work his way down the creek to their camp. That evening when the others returned, Hooper wasn't there. Nor did he come back that night.

In the morning, the fishermen began a search. One man started from where Hooper had been dropped off the previous day, and retraced the route back toward camp.

Nothing in the calm of the morning hinted at the tragedy that had occurred in the area a scant 15 hours earlier. The stream's clear water sparkled merrily over the rocks and pebbles. The man, searching for his buddy, walked in and out of the shadows cast by the tall spruce against the bright September sun. Then he noticed something at the edge of the creek. It was Hooper. Horrified, the man saw that the body was headless.

When the RCMP and Ranger Gerald Stuart from Cadomin arrived at the scene of the tragedy, they found Hooper's body sitting in the creek with the shoulders against the bank. The detached head was in the water. The torso had been disemboweled.

Later that day, Stuart, along with Edson Fire Control Officer Carl Larson, and Edson Ranger Charlie Clark, set out to find the killer animal. The packed gravel of the creek bank left no evidence as to whether a bear or a cougar had done the killing. Larson and Stuart followed a seismic line, not sure at the time what they were looking for.

Clark climbed a nearby ridge. Stuart took an alternate route that would eventually bring the men together again. Within eight yards of their crossing paths, Stuart saw Clark suddenly twist around and fire his rifle, scarcely taking time to aim. His bullet killed a scrawny two-year-old runt bear which had obviously intended a malicious attack on Clark. A sixth sense born of years of hunting had caused him to check over his shoulder and save his life.

The bear was so small that none of the forest officers credited it with being the killer. But they had to be sure. Stuart cut the animal open and took out the stomach. Inside he could feel a lump. Opening the stomach, he found the evidence that showed the hunt was over: a ball of hair and a piece of plaid cloth similar to the shirt worn by Hooper.

Reflecting on the reason for the bear's two unprovoked attacks on humans, the rangers attributed it to the animal's small size and consequent inability to bring down big game. Frustrated, it had settled instead for a smaller and weaker prey, man.

AFS lookoutmen have also had their share of bear confrontations. In one case a lookoutman was unable to return to his lookout from a trip to his privy because a grizzly and her cubs were sunning themselves in front of the lookout cabin.

Two years later, at the same lookout, another towerman was baking bannock when a grizzly appeared. Apparently the culinary fragrance proved irresistible to the bear and it reached up and punched in a window. It did no further damage, but the bear's enthusiastic appreciation of the towerman's cooking discouraged the cook from making any more bannock for the rest of the day.

Another towerman, Albert Popvin, used to sneak into the woods between radio schedules (skeds) to shoot spruce grouse. To be sure he was back in time for the next sked, he carried an alarm clock. When the alarm went off, he had 20 minutes to get back to his cabin. One day he ran into one of the notorious giant Swan Hills grizzlies. Dropping the alarm clock, he headed for the nearest tree. The bear, out of curiosity, hung around, and Popvin could see himself having some explaining to do when he missed the radio sked. Worried and frightened, Popvin peered down at the bear wishing it would go away. At that moment, the alarm rang. The sudden jangle surprised the bear so much it ran off. After recovering his courage, Albert climbed down, headed home on the double and arrived in time for the radio sked.

FIFTEEN

JUMPING POUND

"You got grease?"

Eventually the Forestry thought I had been at Lynx Creek long enough, and they moved me to the Jumping Pound District, 35 miles west of Calgary. I arrived at my new location in the early summer.

Jumping Pound was a job promotion for me, and the many trappings of the station compared to those of Lynx Creek showed this. The dwelling was a full sized log house with an office, a proper chimney, and a basement. The office was equipped with a desk, typewriter and FM radio.

The barn, newer and much better built than the one at Lynx Creek, had five stalls. A team of heavy horses waited in the corral. A wagon, sleigh, mower, hay rake and stoneboat were in the barnyard. Attached to the cache (storehouse) was a shop equipped with forge, anvil and blacksmith tools. A bunkhouse in which the lookout man stayed during the winter stood back among the trees. Best of all was an International half-ton truck sitting in the yard. Dot and I were mobile!

Dot was particularly happy about the move, living so close to Calgary where her parents and sisters lived, and even a truck to take us there.

However, she didn't see her family as much as she had hoped. One reason was that the "road" between us and the nearest municipal highway was 10 miles of dirt track. Many years of wagon wheels (mostly Indians') and occasional truck wheels had worn from the soil a dubious road of their own creation. This discouraged visits from Calgary by Dot's parents except in very benign weather. The other reason was that I had to keep book on every mile I drove the Forestry truck, and none of them were allowed for such frivolous reasons as driving to Calgary for a visit. Although I had to take my reports into Headquarters once a month, and do our grocery shopping, Dot seldom accompanied me as she was pregnant again. She was afraid the rough ride would cause a miscarriage. Anyway, I was never in the city long enough to allow a proper visit.

The Jumping Pound Ranger Station location and area were not as beautiful as Lynx Creek. Consisting largely of second-growth pines and poplars, it lacked spaciousness and high rolling foothills. As there were no large elk herds nor loggers living on remote hillsides that I could visit, game patrol did not provide the enjoyment it had in previous winters. Unfortunately, I had little to do that winter but game patrol.

Curiously, although my status had increased a notch on the promotional grid, I had much less responsibility at Jumping Pound. One logging camp (and even it folded a few months after my arrival) and the cattle grazing were the only commercial activities in the district. This meant, of course, there were no companies maintaining the roads. We were snowed-in all winter.

The stock rider was less efficient than Judge, and did much of his "riding" by pickup truck. A few wealthy, old-time ranch families headed the stock association in that area. They seemed to have a clout that went beyond my authority. I had run-ins with these ranchers while attempting to uphold the government regulations. Unfortunately, head office was loath to clash with them.

Although my responsibility was less, the amount of physical work awaiting me that first summer was not. Part of the telephone line in my district stretched from the ranger station to the provincial telephone hookup at the Indian village of Morley. A good deal of this part of the line ran across open prairie, and many telephone poles needed replacing. So I spent days hauling poles by team and wagon, digging holes and "planting" telephone poles. Large rocks under the soil had to be pried out when I was digging. By the time each hole was deep enough to erect a pole, it was so wide I could bury a horse in it. When I planted poles close to the road, Dot and Camie often accompanied me in the truck. Although Dot was four months pregnant by then, she helped me by holding the poles in place while I threw in rocks and dirt.

Author and son Cam at Jumping Pound Ranger Station

Next to the Morley Indian trading post, the Forestry had an outcabin and stable. With the team, I took a wagonload of telephone poles along the trail, dropping off a pole at each location. Staying overnight at the Morley cabin, I worked my way home next day, planting poles along the way.

Once I came across a young Indian lad looking dolefully at his horse mired in the muskeg. How the horse and rider had slipped off a well-corduroyed trail, I never did find out. The poor animal had given up the struggle and would soon die as horses tend to do when they are down and unable to get off their backs. However, my team pulled the saddle pony out, and it stood shaking and wild-eyed,but safe.

The Stoney Indians were interesting neighbours. Each year, during the Calgary stampede and at other times, too, they made a trip to the city. Their trail to Calgary passed through our barnyard and within a few wagon lengths of our house.

At the head of the procession rode the men on horseback. Following them were buggies and wagons containing women, small children, food, tepee poles and utensils. We always knew a procession of Indians was coming when the two men in the lead arrived at our house. The procession would stop. The remainder of the entourage was so long it spread far back down the road, beyond the barn and out of sight among the trees. Invariably the two leaders got down off their horses, knocked on the door and asked for "grease." The request was always the same.

"You got grease?"

What they meant was, "Do you have anything at all you can spare?"

One day, while I was talking to one of them, I fished out my tobacco and began filling my pipe. There was an immediate response from the Indian.

"You got tobacco?"

I passed him my pouch. He hesitated a moment, then, "You got pipe?"

Once Dot heard them coming when she was out by the barn, but she didn't have time to get back to the house. As she was wearing shorts and a scanty top, she hid behind some logs I had piled before peeling them for telephone poles. She would have been all right if our dog hadn't given her away.

The two Indians followed the snitching dog to where Dot was squatting down in the obvious position of concealment. Without displaying any surprise or amusement, they solemnly asked her if she had any grease.

Another time, Camie and Dot answered a knock on the door to find two Indians asking for the ubiquitous grease. Camie took a puzzled look at the dark-skinned natives, gazed up at Dot and asked, "Mommy, why do they have peanut butter on their faces?"

On 22 November, our second son, Jim, was born in Calgary at the General Hospital. Dot brought him home when he was two weeks old. I thought nothing of it then, but in retrospect I shiver to think of being snowed-in all winter with a new baby and a small child.

Some stresses presented themselves at Jumping Pound, most of them created or compounded by our having no easy access to town in the winter.

In January, I cut myself and contracted blood poisoning which crept up my leg at an alarming rate. I phoned a doctor in Calgary, and told him my condition, and he said to come in immediately.

I drove the five miles to the only logging camp on the district to ask Arnold Schuechner, the superintendent, for help with a logging truck to get to the city. Arnold, a fervent born-again Christian, and ever an optimist, held no doubts about our safely making the trip to Calgary.

"My sister spent Christmas here," he said. "She's a school teacher, and has to be back to work on Monday. I was going to take her in tomorrow anyway, but we'll go in a day early instead. The recent snowfall may cause some trouble, but we'll make it."

Soon Arnold's logging truck drew up at our house. In the cab was Arnold, his sister and one of the crew.

We set off, Arnold's truck breaking trail while Dot, the kids and I followed in our pickup. Outside, the air was still and cold, - 30 degrees F. This kind of cold makes trees resound like shotgun blasts, the kind of cold that quickly punishes the unwary and the unwise.

The snow was deep. Arnold bucked the worst drifts by slamming his truck into them, and grinding on until the truck could go no farther. Then he backed out and hit them again. No football team fought to gain yards more than we did. Following in Arnold's wake, I tried not to think of how we would manage with a small child and a baby if Arnold got in so deep he couldn't back out. We were not near any ranches where we could get help.

Then the unthinkable happened. Arnold's truck broke down. He looked desultorily under the hood, but the weather was too cold to do a proper post-mortem. Quickly we squeezed the teacher into our cab along with Dot, the two children and me. Arnold and his crewman rode outside in the back of the truck.

We drove on for a few minutes until a banging on the cab roof stopped me. "We can't stand the cold out here," cried Arnold.

I got out and let him drive, and soon saw what he meant as my fingers, toes and cheeks began to tingle. Within a very short time, the other man banged on the roof, and Arnold had to get out to let him drive. This musical chairs activity carried on mile after mile as we lurched through the snow drifts.

Then my truck chains began to break – not once, but several times. We can thank God that by then our route ran alongside a rancher's fence. Taking turns cutting the wire, we worked the barbs off with pliers, and joined the breaks in the chain. I was sure the rancher would not have objected to our damaging his fence if he had known our position.

As we took turns holding the pliers and handling the wire, the cold caused our fingers to seize up so we could scarcely move them. Whenever one of us had his turn with this chore, he immediately graduated to the driver's position so he could thaw out. In this way we slowly put the miles behind us – changing drivers and mending truck chains.

I can't describe the relief we all felt when we finally reached Springbank Road, a ploughed secondary highway. We were able to stop a passing truck and obtain a ride for our frozen comrades in the cargo of our truck.

I spent some time recuperating from my blood poisoning in Calgary. Then Dot and I bought enough groceries to last us the remainder of the winter, and headed for home. While still on Springbank Road, which was extremely icy, we slipped off into the ditch. By the time I borrowed a team of horses from a local rancher to pull us out, our groceries in the open back of the truck had frozen solid.

We lived all winter on thawed-out rations.

It is interesting that egg yolks that have been frozen retain their roundness and become hard after they have thawed. Even cooking doesn't soften them. At least, that was our experience.

Later, in the same month, our well dried up. Few things are more alarming than being faced with a family's daily need for water when there is no water source to rely on. We used the snow in the yard for washing and cooking. The only resource left to us for drinking and Jim's formula was Jumping Pound Creek, more than a quarter of a mile away, I had to ride on a trail buried in snow as deep as a horse's chest.

Each day I rode to the creek and back again with a large cream can across my legs. Until a path was well trampled, my horse leaped the depths of snow like a grasshopper in a wheat field. This caused the cream can to bounce and come down heavily on my thighs.

That early spring I attended a five-week course at the Banff School of Fine Arts on the study of wildlife. The lookoutman took me by team and sleigh to Morley where I caught the train to Banff. To attend the course, I had to leave Dot and the children snowed in. However, they were in little danger as the lookoutman, who lived with us during the winter, was an excellent teamster, and could have got the family the 12 miles to the Morley Indian Reserve in an emergency. As I look back, I can see how lonely Dot must have been while I was away. How the weeks must have dragged while she was shut in that snowbound cabin with two very young children.

From 6 February to 11 March, thirty-eight men took part in classes at the Banff School of Fine Arts. The curriculum was sponsored by the Federal Parks and the Alberta Forest Service. Attending were fifteen rangers, nineteen park wardens and four private individuals, (who must have paid a mint for tuition, board and room for all that time.)

The school was the first of its kind. At different stages in the course, 31 professionals and technicians took part as lecturers. They were drawn from the universities of Alberta and British Columbia, the National Parks Service, the Dominion Forest Service, the Alberta Forest Service, the RCMP, the Federal Forest Entomology Branch, the Fire Research Committee, the Federal Department of Mines and Resources and the Vancouver museum. These men were professors, forest superintendents, park superintendents, a policeman, a radio technician, a forest entomologist, a museum curator and a professional ski instructor. Some specialists were internationally known in their respective disciplines.

They took us through a comprehensive study and field work of ungulates (animals with hooves, e.g. deer), fur bearers, fish, birds and other animals.

I left for home the day after the course ended. Getting off the train at Morley, I skied back to my family with skis I had bought in Banff. What a sight to see them at the door, waiting to greet me! I felt I had been away for a year.

The snow was deep the spring my father came to visit. I met him with the team and sleigh when he got off the train at Morley –

twelve snow-packed, trackless miles from the ranger station. The ride home was an experience Dad probably remembered for a long time. He never liked to see animals abused, neglected or even made uncomfortable. That team of horses laboured, knee deep in snow, more than horses are normally expected to work. On the wind-glazed side hills, the sleigh sometimes slid down sideways, producing a thrilling ride for Dad and me and threatening to pull the horses off their feet. I think Dad had been expecting a smooth sleigh ride behind a pair of trotting horses on a level, ploughed country road. He was in his sixties then, and I admired his ability to easily adjust to the hardships of our way of life during his vacation.

One spring day, the superintendent of the Calgary office asked me if I would take part in a movie to be produced by the National Film Board. Naturally I jumped at the chance. The purpose of the film was to show what the *Eastern Rockies Forest Conservation Board* was doing to protect the watershed for future generations of Canadians.

The story was seen through the eyes of two forest rangers: the old-timer who had lived on the eastern slopes for 25 years, and the young ranger who is "gazing into the future" for the next generation.

Bill Shankland, who was in charge of the Bragg Creek District, adjoining the south end of mine, was the old-timer. The crown of his Stetson pushed out into a cone as many old-timers wore their hats, and with his big moustache only inches above the buttons of his uniform, Bill looked every inch the part he was playing. In fact, he *was* the part. So was I in my role of the young, relatively inexperienced ranger. We, along with the film director, Lawrence Cherry and his assistant, Peter Aykroyd, spent most of the summer "on location" in various places in the foothills and mountains. Between changes of locations, I returned to the ranger station for a few days' rest with my family.

Cherry shot his opening scenes on the Cross A-7 Ranch at Lundbreck where he could photograph cattle on the range. He would never shoot unless the sky consisted of the perfect combination of blue firmament and cumulus cloud. As a result, we spent days hanging around places. Once we were four days in a tent in Banff National Park playing cards while the vault of heaven tried to make up its mind. We also hung out at the Willow Creek Ranger Station for about the same amount of time. The incumbent ranger, Jack, a bachelor, made his own beer and was quite generous with it. I think he was overwhelmed by all the company in his secluded life.

During the shooting of the film, Dot was once again left for long periods. She must have been lonely, but she never complained.

The 20 minute film, *Water for the Prairies*, shot in Technicolor, was shown by request at various outdoor association meetings. Some theatre audiences saw it as a trailer included with the main feature. My father and mother saw it at a theatre in Brandon.

Either the Jumping Pound team had been poorly broken as harness horses, or they were not used enough. They continually wanted to be on the run. I was forever sawing on their mouths to keep them to a walk. Even at the end of a day when I walked behind them the one-mile back to the barn, I had to tug and pull at the lines every step of the way. Inevitably, their tendency to run lead to an accident.

One day I finished all my mowing, and drove home on the mower to exchange it for the hay rake. Unhooking the horses from the mower, I hooked them to the rake. Climbing onto the seat, I was

Jumping Pound Ranger Station

about to drive off when Dot called to me from the doorway of the house. Leaning forward, I relaxed the grip of the reins to hear what she had to say. The moment the horses felt the release of my control over them, they reared up, snapping the tongue of the rake and dumping me on the ground. Then they were gone! When I finally caught them, I found they had badly damaged the harness.

I was enraged at the horses, and felt no punishment was too much for them. But it's impossible to punish a horse for running away. Fixing the harness was a major job that took me the rest of that following winter. Each time I worked on it, I became angry with the team again.

I believe all horses are connivers by nature. When you turn a horse out after a day's work, his first thought after he has had a roll is to fill his belly. This will generally take him until dark. Then while he is resting, he is formulating a scheme in which he can get out of work. Or perhaps annoy his human in some way, like standing on his human's foot, and resisting all efforts to push him off. When you want to catch him in the morning, he will let you get right up to him. The second you try to slip the halter on, he nonchalantly walks away, nibbling grass as he goes, just to aggravate you.

**

Eventually progress in the shape of oil caught up to the rangers. "Black gold" became a source of great wealth for the Alberta government, and this was reflected in many changes to the Alberta Forest Service.

In the reserves governed by the *Eastern Rockies Forest Conservation Board*, the government burned the ancient log ranger cabins. They were replaced with frame houses complete with running water and gasoline generated electric power. Soon every ranger was issued a truck, and an edict went out that patrols and business were no longer to be done on horseback. This caused a few old timers to hand in their resignations. FM radios replaced the old SPF-AM radios and the telephone tree-line. Helicopters and airborne fire-bombers made the fire trails obsolete.

Finally, the rangers moved into the towns, and the comparatively new, white frame houses were torn down or burned. The term *ranger* was changed to *forest officer,* and the incumbents became specialists. That is, the old ranger districts now have an individual looking after the range, another concerned with the lumber and oil industry, another with wildlife, and so on. All these professionals together do what used to be the job of one man. Thus in the interests of greater efficiency in an expanding and busier population, the romance of the job that had been inherently a part of it since 1888 was taken away.

Dot and I and the two children were also affected by these great changes. In 1950 we moved to Calgary.

Sixteen

HINTON

The opportunity to return to the bush was overwhelming

For almost five years Dot, the two boys and I lived in Calgary. We bought a lot on Calgary's north western outskirts near the foot of prominent Nose Hill. Today that area is a sea of houses, but in the early 1950's our street was on the city's northern boundary, and we looked out on prairie.

Dot was now able to be in daily contact with her parents and both sisters; she enjoyed all the city amenities in a new house. She was happy. However, I chafed under the regular working hours and the traffic. I missed the quietness of the forest, the snowshoe patrols on the hillsides of deep snow, the saddle horse excursions along the mountain trails. I had trouble adjusting to city streets.

After buying an old Ford car for $100, we often drove out in the summer to Jumping Pound and picnicked beside the creek. In the winter, we coaxed our ancient vehicle down country roads until we came to reasonably remote spots where we could light a fire in the snow, have a lunch and snowshoe around.

I longed so much for the bush life that I wrote my Forestry experiences and sold them as a 3-part series to the Winnipeg Free Press Prairie Farmer. This was my first attempt at writing, and my immediate success in being published encouraged me to write for other publications. Soon I was into a new hobby. I wrote about trapping, forest ranging, logging camps, pack rats, timber cruising, the symbiotic relationship of water and trees, the Ten Year Cycle and other related subjects. I sold my articles to the *Calgary Herald, Canada Lumberman, Family Herald, Toronto Star Weekly, B.C. Outdoors, Western Producer* and others.

Somehow the writing helped to keep my frustrations at a level I could handle.

One day I received a letter from Des Crossley, a Federal Government forester I knew. "You will be surprised," he wrote, "to learn I have accepted the position of chief forester for Alberta's first pulpmill, in Hinton. I will be looking for timber cruisers, Robin, and I am wondering if you would be interested."

This opportunity to return to the bush was almost overwhelming. I talked it over with Dot. Typically, she unselfishly hid her reluctance at leaving her house, parents and new friends, and encouraged me to take the job.

As a result, one day in April I boarded a bus to Hinton. Turning at Edmonton, we headed west on highway 16, currently paved and 4-lanes, but in 1955 only a gravel road. With mixed feelings, I watched the scenery pass by. I was glad to be headed back to the bush and new experiences. But was I doing the right thing by my family? Dot was five months pregnant, with two small boys to look after. Was this compulsion of mine to get out of the city at all costs unreasonable and irrational? My conscience began to bother me, and this took away from the excitement of a new adventure.

Eventually we pulled up at the Hinton Hotel, incongruously sitting on the edge of nowhere. When the passengers stepped from the bus, we could see the "old" Hinton: a general store, a service station, and here and there a few cabins.

Also visible, a mile away, was the "new" Hinton in the beginning of her birth pains. Concrete and steel understructures and frameworks marked the beginning of Alberta's first multimillion dollar pulpmill. Alongside the construction were bunkhouses for 800 labourers and tradesmen.

That evening I walked around the noisy, dusty, busy settlement. There was an air of expectancy and excitement that must have paralleled Juneau and Nome during the Klondike gold rush days. The din of racing Letourneaus and earth-gouging bulldozers was everywhere as men and machines levelled the mill site, the size of one and a half football fields. Competing in the general racket were huge "cats," road packers and an army of men who were laying out the ribbon of roadbed that was to become the approach to the new Hinton. With barely enough time to straighten up between jobs the owner/ mechanic in Hinton's only garage was overloaded with a bewildering number of vehicles needing repairs. The general store seemed to be always sold out of something as dozens of men bought writing paper, tobacco and socks. The Bank of Nova Scotia had established itself by hauling a rough lumber shack on skids near the store, sticking a sign over the door and opening for business in good old boomtown style. Next door, a man and his wife were selling mens' clothing out of another shack that had been thrown together in a hurry, and a lean-to hardware store was being built beside it.

I tried to buy myself a glass of beer but couldn't get into the beer parlour. I could hear the clinking coins and clanking glasses as the waiters rushed from table to fountain and back. Packed full, and with a line-up outside waiting for a vacant chair, the place was a hornet's nest of incessant noise. In the lobby of the hotel a line of men waited to use the hamlet's only telephone.

On the next day I met the other timber cruisers. I soon learned that cruising timber for industry was more technical, specific and much more accurate than the "ocular" timber cruising I used to do for the government. In the old days, the rangers walked without a planned route through the bush, and *guestimated* the amount of timber there was in the given area. In later years, the Forest Service held schools that taught proper cruising within plots, 32 feet in diameter, or along a uniform width on each side of an imaginary line. But I never got to one of those schools. So I had to quickly learn a more precise method of cruising timber. We counted every tree in each plot and recorded its species. We found tree ages by boring into them with an increment borer and withdrawing a core of wood on which we counted the rings. We took accurate tree height measurements with Abney hand levels that employed geometric laws to gauge the tree lengths. Using callipers, we measured at breast height the diameters of trees.

From such accurate measurements we gathered detailed data from which the company's planners computed timber volume. This allowed them to view the forests, not as a scattered collection of trees, but as rectangular blocks representing a number of cubic feet of wood per acre of forest. From this information, management devised programmes of cutting and reforestation including where to put the camps of pulpwood cutters, how big each camp should be, and where to leave parent tree stands for regeneration.

There were seven of us, and each took his turn staying at camp to cook, while the others took to the bush for the day. Working in pairs, our life was rugged as we followed our compass needles. We couldn't deviate from the direction of our cruise line, and it often pointed across muskegs, impenetrable new growth, lakes, steep hills and windfall. Cruising for one year with scarcely a break, we had to fight mosquitoes, lightning storms, rain, freezing weather and deep snow. Only a person who has had to pull himself away from the relative comfort of a midday outdoor lunch fire in 30 below zero weather and plunge into the frigid air to follow a cruise line can appreciate the old-time timber cruiser's life.

Sometimes we stumbled upon some history of this romantic country. An old road barely discernible, a deserted coal mine miles from any modern transportation facilities, a disintegrating trapper's cabin: these are the fading links with yesterday's pioneers that we ran across during our timber cruises. Two miles into the forest off Highway 16 near Jasper Park's east gate, sits the Grand Trunk Railway Station of *Park Gate*. The old building was forgotten until we discovered it during a timber cruise. A rare phenomenon, drifting sand from the bottom of nearby Brulc Lake, made railroading impossible in this area. Bit by bit, the sand washed up from the waters to move with the wind, filling the station house until its walls buckled and its roof lifted. The nearby old telegraph poles were buried to within six feet of their tops. In 1928, the sand had eventually forced the railway company to move its steel across the lake.

The company issued us a large tent, individual folding cots, the best of sleeping bags, a Jeep and all the food we could eat – mostly tinned goods as few of us cared to cook. Despite our Arctic down bags, we were cold as the folding cots allowed the cold mountain air to assault us from underneath. The company replaced the cots with air mattresses but found that they were only marginally warmer. Foam rubber was either not invented then or not common. I remembered spruce boughs as the warmest mattress one could have outdoors, and occasionally I cut myself some.

Considering how closely we lived together, we seven cruisers were reasonably compatible. Slugging through deep snow all day long was hard work, but we made a joke of it. We pretended we were members of a local snowshoe club going for a "snowshoe ride". We stayed in the bush five days each week. On Saturday mornings we all climbed into our company Jeep and returned to Hinton for rejuvenation

As our cruises penetrated deeper into the wilderness, we had to keep moving camp. Sometimes we bounced along in our jeep on old logging roads that had become deeply rutted and eroded, barricaded with windfall, or terminated at a washed-out bridge. Occasionally one of these roads lead to a deserted logging camp. We then moved our gear into the best building, usually the kitchen, and made it liveable by boarding up the broken windows and cleaning out the packrats' nests. Other times we were forced to winch ourselves in the Jeep as far as we could, then pack our grub, equipment and bedding on our backs to where we had decided to erect our tent.

Eventually we reached the Yellowhead Cabin, the Forestry outcamp at which I had found such perfect solitude when I was assistant ranger at Coalspur. I endured some strong poignant feelings during our stay there. There was no solitude with that crowd of shouting, excitable characters. Although the cabin looked the same, the narrow, secluded pack trails leading to it had become rough logging roads. I missed the bugling of the elk, the horse in the corral and the peaceful, gentle evenings I had known at this spot ten years previously.

All the cruisers were married, and our wives had been left behind in their respective homes. Dot had the responsibility of selling our house on her own. This involved a certain amount of painting and making the house as saleable as she could.

In August, she and the two boys arrived on a weekend visit. I found room in a big ranch house to put them up.

"There will be houses here, Dot, with running water and electric lights," I told her. "There will be streets and avenues and shops and theatres."

But Dot looked at the virgin forest and didn't believe me. Seven months pregnant, she returned to Calgary, a sad and frightened girl faced with the prospect of returning to a hard life in the bush. On 30 September 1955, our daughter, Nancy, was born at the Holy Cross Hospital in Calgary. For the third time I had missed the opportunity of being available during the birth of one of my children. However, I was not going to make the mistake I did at Campbell's entrance into the world, sending laundry in a flower box. I wired a florist in Calgary to make up a large basket of gladiolus, the flowers we had at our wedding.

But again I blew it. The hospital had been so full that Dot had been put into a room with three women whose babies had been born out of wedlock. These mothers were going to give their babies away, and it was a sad place in which there was little cause for celebrating. Dot felt both embarrassed and out of place among the three unfortunate women when the big basket of flowers was presented to her.

During a weekend in Hinton, I wrote an article describing the impact that North Western Pulp & Power was having on Hinton and eventually on Alberta. The Calgary Herald bought it, and printed it on their editorial page.

The story came to the attention of *North Canadian Oils*, *North Western's* Canadian partner. President Frank Ruben clipped it and sent it to the senior partner in New York: St. Regis Paper Company.

Soon after, I received a packet in the mail from St. Regis' vice-president of public relations. In it was a letter saying he had made a general bulletin of my article and was sending it to the 800 members of St. Regis' organization throughout North America. Enclosed also was an advance copy of the general bulletin headed: *New Pulpmill Transforms Hamlet Into Boom-town*.

I was surprised that such a small and insignificant piece of writing should seem so important, but it gave me a big lift.

Soon after this, our cruising party moved to a camp on the far side of Brule Lake, actually a widening of Athabasca River. One evening

Tom Lewko, company clerk, drove out from Hinton with orders for me to accompany him back to the office. This entailed a boat trip across the lake, a 4-wheel-drive journey of about five miles on a rough bush road, and about 14 miles on the highway. When we arrived, I met St. Regis' vice-president of public relations, Ken Lozier. He had wanted to meet the author of that article. What he said amazed me. "In time, North Western will be needing a public relations manager. We'll be keeping our eyes on you."

That was all he said, and Tom drove me back to the cruisers' bush camp. He left with barely enough daylight to get his boat back across the water as he made his way home after dropping me off.

With the coming of fall, the company located some old tourist cabins, and dragged them in to be used during the winter so we could bring our wives to Hinton. Because Dot and I had the most children, we were given two cabins attached to each other. I punched a hole in the adjoining wall of each so there was free entry from one cabin to the other. One warm early September weekend saw all of us building closed-in porches onto our cabins with lumber the company had bought for us.

At Christmas I returned to Calgary to be with the family and to move our furniture to Hinton. Dot had sold the house and we had to be out of it shortly after New Year's Day. Using a truck North Western had lent me, I returned, alone, with our furniture and our Boxer dog, Koko. The day after I got to Hinton, I spent in the office working on some maps, and left Koko by herself in our cabin. When I got home at the end of the day, I found that she had chewed an arm off the sofa. She had never done any chewing or damage before, and I knew that she was having some deep set psychological problem from being left alone in a strange house filled with familiar furniture. I didn't punish her or even chastise her, but the next day I took her with me when I went out into the field again.

Koko was the first dog to live in the "new" Hinton. Because she was the only dog for a time, and because of her quiet and friendly manner, children took to her. Indicative of her popularity was the fact that in Hinton some youngsters' first word was – not "Mommy" or "Daddy" – but "Koko."

Meanwhile, the wives of the management and clerical personnel had begun appearing. When Dot and the children arrived in January, there were twelve families set up in their tourist cabins for the winter.

That fall, we all banked our cabins with gravel, filled our propane tanks, and shouting, "Do your worst, Winter," crawled into our cabins and bolted our doors against the onslaught.

Why Old Man Winter took a dislike to these forerunners of North Western Pulp & Power is not known. He dug down into his deep-freeze, brought up the coldest temperatures he could find, and deposited them right into that little camp.

That stirred things up. The propane in the big cylinders behind each cabin congealed. The fires went out and the families awoke and were unable to get back to sleep because of the cold. Many nights the men crawled out of bed at two or three o'clock to light wood fires under their propane tanks to get the propane circulating again. Occasionally, with no heat in the cabin, we ate breakfast dressed in parkas. Winter struck again and again.

An unfortunate decision of North Western Pulp & Power Ltd. was to dig our sewer and water lines two feet deep. Naturally they froze with the first serious frost, and never thawed until spring. Some pipes broke, and the sewers backed up into the cabins. Stan Hart, Assistant Woodlands Manager, ushered in the new year by digging up his sewer pipes to seal them off. Because our water lines were frozen, the company issued each family a 5-gallon container that we filled from a truck that delivered water several times a week. The evening moon looked down on the men as they lined up in the dark to draw their ration. As we had three children, we had to be cautious about how we used our water. Often I was forced to go next door and beg a saucepan of water from our neighbours.

The Company's piped-in electricity from a diesel generator wasn't nearly enough to do the job. Our electric lights gave us just enough glow to prevent us from stumbling over the furniture, and appliances didn't function properly.

Then one night Old Man Winter summed up all he had and delivered a smashing blow. The cold broke previous records in that area. The Crossleys' thermometer dropped to 56 degrees below. The Gimbarzevskys' claimed 58 below. The thermometer at the river, which was graduated to 60 degrees, dropped out of sight.

During a visit of Des Crossley's father, his false teeth froze in a glass of water. And Dot, getting out of bed to check on the baby, found her slippers frozen to the floor. It was shortly after this we received a letter from Dad saying he would come for a visit. When he arrived, he spent most of his time huddled around the heater trying to coax a little warmth from it.

By then, the company knew where they wanted to put their first pulpwood cutters' camp. I was taken off timber cruising and given the job of laying out the various areas to be cut for Camp Number One. To lay out the cut areas, I had a map that showed the potential cuts. By using a compass and careful pacing, I located the boundaries and stapled ribbons on the trees to mark them.

I enjoyed this.

Once again I was alone in the bush, snowshoeing in deep snow through virgin forests. It's true I had to follow the direction my compass needle took me, and I wasn't as free as I was as a ranger, but I still felt the same sense of solitude. And even more importantly, this job allowed me to go home to my family every night.

Finally spring arrived. One night, Dot woke up to hear water dripping from the showerhead in the bathroom. She ran into the bathroom, turned on the water, then raced back to wake me. "We have running water again," she shouted.

My days of bush travel were ending. The construction of the mill was nearing completion, Camp Number One was built, and it was time to get some men into the bush cutting pulpwood.

Key mill personnel were making an appearance. A resident manager/ vice-president by the name of Tom Easley had been hired. Also a personnel manager came on the scene.

Not long after that I was given the job of hiring pulpwood cutters. My title was employment supervisor, and my boss was the personnel manager.

SEVENTEEN

OUTDOOR OPPORTUNITIES

The family took advantage of the outdoor opportunities

"This is your bailiwick," said the personnel manager, showing me an empty building. "You'll have a secretary, and your job will be to hire as many pulpwood cutters as you can as fast as you can. If you need me, I'll be in the main building."

In my new job as employment supervisor, the first thing I did was to flood all the western rural newspapers with advertisements calling for pulpwood cutters. The result was a deluge of applicants standing at my door, filling the hallway and wandering around outside the building.

In my ignorance, I thought the hiring procedure required a formal interview. Therefore, I instructed my secretary, Freddie, to go through the dog-and-pony show of bringing each *wanabe* pulpwood cutter into my office so I could interview him and his qualifications. That ridiculous procedure resulted in my falling behind in my quota of daily hiring, which did not sit well with the management of the Woodlands Division. Perceiving that this was not the way to hire men for the bush, I changed tactics.

Squeezing ten men at a time into my office, I asked only two questions:

1. "Who has had experience falling trees?" The few who admitted to not having a previous bush background were rejected. 2. "Who has his own saw, axe and equipment?" Those

who did not have tools were rejected. The remainder were given medicals and sent to a camp.

Senior management was now satisfied with my daily quotas. However, a new problem developed. As many men were quitting as I was hiring. When new men entered the camps, they passed men who were on their way out.

In search of reasons for the quits, Freddie and I quickly went through their applications for some common denominators.

We found two:

1. All those who were trying to earn a living with a swede saw were giving up after two or three days. No one could possibly survive at the production rate we demanded unless he had a power saw.

2. The greatest number of quits by far were Albertans. They were not used to a high-powered, disciplined daily grind in the bush. Alberta tree fallers were used to working for the little "gypo"[5] companies that dotted the eastern slopes of the Rocky Mountain foothills. Their pace was much slower. They had managed with swede saws and cross-cut saws, and they had not had to compete with high wage earners.

From then on, the applicants from Ontario had top priority. And no one without a chain saw stood a donkey's chance of being taken on.

About two months after I began hiring pulpwood cutters, the vice president fired the personnel manager, and I suddenly found myself in his job. Under the industrial relations manager, I was now responsible for hiring mill workers and all office people except management personnel. Now, someone else, responsible to me, hired the pulpwood cutters.

I also found I was ultimately in charge of the security police and the company's fire department. These men took their orders directly from a lanky, good-natured man whom I nicknamed "Cabbagehead" because of his belief in boiled cabbage as the only way to good health and long life. He seemed to like his new name.

A few months later, the vice-president fired the public relations manager. (It seemed no one's head was safe in this company.) Public relations was a senior management job in which a mistake in proto-

---

[5] **a small contractor**

col or sensitive information could damage the company's reputation. I didn't expect for one minute I would be promoted into this position. I didn't even think about it, and I certainly didn't apply for it. To my great surprise – *to my amazement* – the VP offered me the job.

I now sat on the policy-making board of twelve department heads chaired by the resident manager/vice president. With a relatively luxurious office next to his, I felt as if I had been appointed to the senate. It wasn't as cushy a job as many of my old bush cohorts thought.

Soon after the appointment to my new position, the resident manager called me into his office.

"I have a big job for you, Robin. The mill start-up is approaching, and we must be prepared to introduce ourselves and our product to the people of Alberta and to the pulp consumers in North America. At the risk of sounding like a radio commercial, I remind you that we are the first pulpmill in Alberta and the province's largest industrial operation. Our process is the most up-to-date in the world. At this time, we are the most modern pulpmill on the globe, and our product will be without comparison."

I nodded.

"I want you to spearhead a celebration to proclaim our formal opening. I will tell you later whom to invite. Our guests will be the top people in the Alberta government and industry, both in Canada and the USA. Our celebration will be a visible exposition of the friendship and community of interest between the two countries."

My head was swirling. "Will I have help, Tom?"

"You may ask anyone you want for help. If you meet any resistance, tell me about it. Form a committee to advise you. And use only top men; if you need something to be done, the people on your committee must have the authority to push it through."

"What about money?"

"Initially you will be operating on a budget of $64,000. Keep me posted daily on what you are doing, and be prepared to report to our weekly board meeting. Let me leave you with this thought, Robin. *Be sure this party has a happy ending. It is extremely important that our guests carry away positive memories of their stay with us.*"

But forming a committee wasn't so easy. Top management in the Engineering, Production and Accounting Departments pleaded "too busy getting ready for start-up," and wanted to delegate junior people to take their places. So I tried my old friends in the Woodlands Division. The head man there told me in typical woodsy fashion that all this "party B.S." was Mill business and had nothing to do with Woodlands.

His answer didn't surprise me. The woodlands manager had been refusing to take orders from the VP/resident manager, claiming that the VP was head of the Mill Division only, and had no jurisdiction over Woodlands. (Actually, the VP was boss over the entire company.)

The woodlands manager's attitude resulted in his being fired by a St.Regis Woodlands vice president who arrived from New York to do the job. He was replaced by Adrian Provencher, a French Canadian with a strong French accent.

Adrian at once agreed to be on my committee. Because of his upbeat attitude and acceptance of the formal opening concept, so did the rest of his top management agree to be part of the committee.

The list of invitees read like a "Whose Who" of industry and government. In fact, that's what it was. Government guests included the Alberta premier and lieutenant-governor, provincial treasurer, and various ministers. Among the top industrial people were St. Regis Paper Company's board chairman, president and executive vice-president; Alberta Wheat Pool's general manager; and presidents of Hudson's Bay Oil and Gas, and the Bank of Nova Scotia – 96 guests altogether.

Many details had to be considered, including the design of the invitation, keeping the guests amused during slack moments, and banquet preparations at Jasper Lodge.

Protocol was one of our biggest problems. We hired most of Jasper town for two days. Who should get the top suites and rooms in the Jasper Park Lodge? Who then will be given quarters in Beckers Bungalows and Tekerra Lodge? The company's department heads, (who were at the bottom of the pecking order) such as myself, were assigned bunks in a railway car we had hired from the CNR.

When I think of the size of the project, which should have been contracted to a professional public relations firm, when I think that the whole thing was left up to a small group of foresters who knew nothing of hoopla and public hootenannies, I am filled with wonder.

When the great day arrived, the weather was on our side. Facing the water on bleachers we had built beside a beautiful little lake, the guests listened to various speakers. The sun shone from a cloudless sky, and five wild ducks, swimming back and forth while gazing at us in curiosity, thrilled the onlookers. Some thought we had arranged for the ducks to be there. The rest of the day was equally successful.

Later in the year, at the suggestion of Chief Forester Des Crossley, I wrote to the Canadian Forestry Association (CFA) for help to organize the Alberta Junior Forest Wardens. Mr. D.C. Powers, of the CFA came from Vancouver to draft a contract in which North Western agreed to sponsor the new group. *Thus, was started the Junior Forest Warden (JFW) movement in Alberta.* In 1960, the Alberta Forest Service took over the JFWs and developed their activities throughout the province.

Meanwhile, bulldozers had cut streets and avenues out of the

Dot, our pet, Koko, and I camped out as often as we could

bush. Houses and shops appeared. Dot and I bought a house across from a woodsy area that had been left undamaged and designated as a park.

During this time, the family was taking advantage of the magnificent outdoor opportunities in the area. Before the appearance of the recreational vehicle, people could camp in government campgrounds at no charge. The campgrounds were quiet places that attracted only true campers. Although a few sleeping shelters on the backs of pickup trucks were beginning to appear, almost everyone tented. There was none of the racket and hoodlumism that is often in today's public campgrounds.

One year, the family explored the old Grand Trunk Railway. From its Park Gate Station, (falling apart under tons of drifting sand from the shores of Brule Lake) to the town of Edson was about 50 miles. I carried Nancy on my back, and the others trailed behind. In the days before children's backpacks, Nancy rode in an old American army packsack with holes cut for her legs to hang out. She had to ride facing backward, but seemed happy in her sedan.

Part of the right-of-way was so grown in we had difficulty locating it. Sometimes, we found it by looking at the tops of the trees; where the line had been cut out years before, a faint opening still showed in places. At other times we scratched through the duff until we came upon old, buried railway ties. Now and then, a still-standing telegraph pole told us we were in the right place. Once we came across a grave of a civil engineer who had died presumably while employed in the building of the railway. We also found ancient train parts and other evidence of a former operating railroad.

The author as personnel manager

Eighteen

ROCK CLIMBING, SPELUNKING AND SKIING

The cave's width extended beyond our flashlights' radius

As the years went by, my responsibilities increased until I was in charge of personnel, public relations, safety, fire protection and security.

Carrying out those duties was far removed from tramping the bush on snowshoes, and I knew I was going to have to spend much of my free time in the bush to endure the pressures of management.

Hinton is only 16 miles from Jasper Park, and if one faces west on the main business street of the Hill townsite, his distant vision will be filled with the many mountain peaks for which Jasper is known. That scene attracted me like a moth to a candle flame. I wanted to get to the tops of those peaks, but I didn't have any knowledge of scaling rock and ice.

However, I soon got to know a man in Jasper who was willing to teach me for a price. Willy Pfisterer was a tough, breezy Austrian who had been born with an ice axe in one hand and a ski pole in the other. He had an interesting Austrian accent, and could attract your attention on the mountains with a clear, echoing yodel that compared in quality to that of cowboy singer Wilf Carter. Years Later, Willy guided Prime Minister Pierre Trudeau on the ascent of Mount Colin across the river from the Jasper airstrip.

To pay the fee Willy asked as guide and instructor, I organized a group of twelve other men and women who thought they might like

Rocky Morin
on Angel Glacier

to scale the peaks too. The thirteen of us learned the mysteries of the mountaineer's rope, and the use of pitons and carabiners. We went out every weekend until we all graduated from "Rock School." After that, four of us went on to take "Ice School" on the glaciers, one of whom was my younger son, Jim.

Only two of us benefited completely from Willy's instruction. Rocky Morin and I continued to climb for years. Together we shared so many weekends exploring the rock and ice between Jasper Gate and the Saskatchewan Glacier that we became close, lifelong friends.

One day, Rocky and I broke camp early at the Columbia Icefields to go up the Athabaska glacier and continue beyond the icefalls to get onto the seven mile wide mass of ice on top, which can't be seen from the highway. As we progressed up the glacier,

at "Ice School"

we encountered snow left over from the previous winter. Knowing the snow lay on top of deep crevasses of ice, we roped up.

That decision saved me from some broken bones and maybe losing my life. As I picked up my backpack, I suddenly plunged straight down through the snow. By instinctively throwing out my arms, I was able to stop my descent into the crevasse. While my arms were spread out like wings on a bird, they gave me buoyancy, and I remained on top of the snow. But I could feel my legs swinging free, and I knew I was in extreme danger of the snow suddenly giving way, allowing me to continue my fall into unknown depths. Rocky jammed his ice axe into the ice (as he was taught at Willy's Ice School), wrapped his climbing rope around it, and gradually, slowly helped me to extricate myself.

Afterwards, Rocky carefully crawled on his stomach to the hole I had made, and looked down. He was able to see many feet below , but was unable to see the bottom of the crevasse.

That incident made me nervous for the rest of the trip, expecting any moment to suddenly fall through another snow bridge.

**

Somehow someone at the university in Edmonton had heard mistakenly that I was an intrepid and experienced mountaineer. As a result, I occasionally was approached by small groups of students asking to come to Hinton for me to take them on small rock climbs. I always obliged as I enjoyed climbing, and liked to have company along, if just for safety's sake.

One morning I took six or seven female students from the university in Edmonton up Mount Morrow, a small 5500 foot summit west of Hinton. When we reached the top, I decided to take them down the back side of the mountain via a deep canyon. We had to descend into the canyon by rappelling and once in, there was no way of climbing back out as the walls were polished smooth by water flow over the years. We walked down the canyon until we came to a 20-foot waterfall.

The last time I had been down the canyon, the waterfalls had held only a trickle of water, and descending them had meant no more than getting a little wet. But his time a torrent of water cascaded over the falls.

The girls wanted to go back, and I had to convince them that the only way they could get home was by going over the waterfall. The reason they didn't mutiny was that they needed me to get them out.

I looped the climbing rope through a piton and tossed it over the rim of the waterfall in preparation for a rappel. Then I rappelled down to show them that it was possible. A heavy splurge of water hit me in the face and up my nose, leaving me gasping for air. I landed in a hollowed out basin of water, two feet deep, at the bottom.

Eventually, all the girls went over the falls, and I watched each one fighting for oxygen, her mouth opening and closing like a fish's as she descended. They didn't like it, but there was no other way.

With drenched feet and clothes , we progressed down the canyon floor. The walls kept getting higher and higher as we came across more waterfalls. We eventually descended the last waterfall, and walked out the bottom of the canyon to our cars parked just off the highway. If I remember correctly, that was the last group of university students who asked me to take them out.

Each year, when the snow came and we could climb no more, we took up our skis. The only lift in Jasper was at Whistler Mountain (not to be confused with the famous Whistler Mountain resort in British Columbia.) In addition to skiing downhill, Rocky and I put climbing 'skins' on our skis and climbed to the 8000 foot Marmot Peak. We usually got only one run down in a day – rarely two, at the most – but it was a good one. Sometimes we were the only skiers on the mountain; now there are lifts and thousands of skiers every weekend testing their mettle on Marmot.

1961 was a good year for our family. That winter saw us regularly making use of Jasper's ski slopes. Everyone in the family, but Dorothy, was eager to glide down snow-covered inclines. As soon as we arrived at the ski chalet, we could barely wait to change from our shoes to our ski boots. Dorothy was a good sport, and put in her time either attacking the bunny slopes on her skis or writing letters in the chalet.

**

One summer, I heard of an enormous cave high on a mountain side above the ghost town of Cadomin in the Coal Branch. Although the cave had existed for many thousands of years, its entrance is so narrow, its locality so remote, through the years only a relatively small number of people could have been in it. No one knows when the cave was first discovered. A prospector from southern Alberta claims he found it more than 50 years before we entered it, and there were probably others before him. (Lately, the provincial government has stepped in and made it a regulated tourist attraction.)

Dexter Champion, the company's Woodlands fire marshall, and Herman Oosterhuis, a company forester, came with me to find this cavern.

After searching, we finally came across the cave's narrow entrance – a mere slit in the rock face. On the seat of my pants, I slid down through the narrow aperture. Bright sunlight suddenly changed to inky blackness. Flicking on my flashlight, I waited in the dank stillness until I heard Dexter and Herman sliding in after me.

Dexter gasped. In all his 20 years as a woodsman he had never seen anything like this. Neither had Herman or I. We were in the largest limestone cave yet discovered in Alberta.

Slowly our flashlight beams swept the cavern. Twenty feet above us on the lumpy ceiling, sharp ledges slashed deeply into the walls. Beneath our feet was a floor of thick silt.

I took the lead as we moved cautiously ahead to where the cavern narrowed intriguingly into a corridor. Herman brought up the rear, feeding out a string from a large roll attached to his belt. This would lead us back to the outside, once we had satisfied our curiosity.

As we progressed, the great room inside the entrance narrowed although the ceiling retained its height. A hundred feet farther on, we found ourselves in a high, narrow corridor. The floor now contained deep crevasses or potholes at the bottom on which jagged rocks awaited the person who lost his footing. At times we had to cling to ledges and examine the floor before each step. Suddenly we began to move downhill, and the corridor ended abruptly at a small opening that we crawled through into another high corridor. Then came our greatest thrill. The passage opened into a huge cavern, the walls of which were pocked with caves. Many of these were big enough to hold two automobiles.

The width of the room extended beyond the range of our two-cell flashlights. Large rocks had crashed down from the walls and from the ceiling 30 feet above. The silence was eerie.

Narrow tunnels led off in every direction, and perhaps went on to other gigantic rooms. The tunnels were too narrow for us, and to investigate them required more nerve than we possessed. We decided not to leave the main cavern.

Before we climbed back to daylight, we had spent two hours in the cave. As we crawled out of the entrance, the July sun felt uncomfortably hot, and momentarily blinded us.

During the next ten years, I visited the cave three more times, each time accompanied by different people.

**

At work, I thought it would be a good idea for the company's fire crews to learn roof rescue. There was not likely to be a great need to rescue someone from a roof, but the fire fighters had reached the zenith of their training, and needed something else to keep their interest from flagging. I hired Willy Pfisterer to come once a week from Jasper, and teach them how to rappel from the mill roofs, and to lower a wounded person down onto the ground. Willy did a good job, and the guys loved the training.

In March of 1962, Willy offered me the opportunity of accompanying him and two clients on an eleven day, 110 mile ski trip across the mountains south of Jasper. I asked if Rocky Morin could come along too, and Willy consented.

This was the time of year when the snow around the town of Jasper was visible only in patches. Along our route, however, it was so deep as to make it impossible to be off our skis except to sleep.

Although the route (Skyline Trail) is popular to high-level summer hikers, according to Willy no one else had ever skied the entire length before.

On the first day, we climbed from Maligne Canyon to Signal Mountain fire lookout south of Jasper. I was challenged to the full extent of my strength and nerve to keep up to these people who had been skiers all their lives, and were 10 to 15 years younger than me.

The next day, we sighted herds of Mountain caribou, a close relative of the Woodlands caribou, but living its life in the snow and rocks above timberline. We also spotted a flock of bighorn sheep, many with three-quarter or fully curved horns. Ptarmigan huddled in the snow, looking like oversize snowballs.

On the third day, we continued until we reached the peak of Sunset Mountain. Overhanging snow cornices indicated avalanche conditions, forcing us to take extreme precautions in some places. Even then, we inadvertently caused two small slides, one of which broke off under Willy's skis.

At one time I fell while negotiating a steep slope. Suddenly I was wallowing in a deep pocket of fluffy powder that clogged my mouth, nose, eyes and ears. My first reaction was to struggle up for air. Then came the lengthy, tiring ordeal of wriggling out of my pack, and somehow getting free of my skis. Impossible to stand without sinking waist deep, I had to climb onto my skis as one might clamber onto a life raft in water. The entire operation of self-rescue was a lengthy struggle, and I was careful after that not to fall again. On the fifth day, we reached Maligne Lake. The next two days found us along Shovel Pass, finally ending on Endless Ridge on days eight and nine. These names will be familiar to those who have hiked the Skyline trail.

At Jonas Pass, we spent most of the eleventh day descending. As we got lower, we came out of powder snow onto ice, and I can remember digging the steel edges of my skis with all my might into the side of the mountain to prevent myself from sliding sideways down the slope at a dangerous speed. Finally, ankles aching, and tired, we came out at Jonas Creek campground on the highway.

I didn't realize how deeply tanned we were until I got back to work and found everyone exclaiming over my russety skin.

**

If you stand on the beach in front of Chateau Lake Louise and look up the lake, your gaze will eventually come to rest on Lower Victoria Glacier. As you allow your scrutiny to continue upwards past the rock and ice, you will see Mounts Lefroy and Victoria, both in excess of 11,000 feet in height.

On the July 1, 1963 weekend a climb to the summit of Mount Victoria was the goal of three aspiring, amateur rock climbers: Rocky Morin, Pete Schopflocher and myself. Pete was another mountain nut who spent too many of his weekends, at all times of the year, on the slopes and heights of the Alberta Rockies.

We bussed into Lake O'Hara, near Field, BC, took a brief look around the beautiful little chateau, turned our backs on the tempting smell of coffee and toast being served up to the patrons, and hit the trail. We spent most of the rest of the day climbing the 3000 feet to Abbot Pass. The last 1500 feet were a chest-heaving slog up an almost vertical slope of rock and scree until we joyfully reached our destination.

Abbot Pass, on the Continental Divide, is a rocky saddle joining the west face of Lefroy with the southeast ridge of Victoria. On one side is British Columbia and on the other side is Alberta. In the middle of the pass, blended with the surrounding rock, is a stone hut where we spent the night.

To learn how the pass got its name, we must go back to August 3, 1896. That was the day Philip Abbot, George Little, Charles Fay and Charles Thomson almost reached the summit of Mount Victoria.

The day was getting late, and although they were only 200 feet from their goal, the sensible thing to do was to turn around and go back before dark caught them stranded on the mountain.

However, Abbot, a 28 year old American lawyer, wasn't about to give in easily. He talked George Little into belaying him as he traversed to a rock gully from which he could get higher. As Little was feeding out rope to him, Abbot's body suddenly passed him in an uncontrolled fall. Abbot struck the icy mountain slope on his head, close to where Thomson and Fay waited. Somehow, and never explained, the rope became unattached from Little, and Abbot's body continued to hurtle down the west face of the mountain. Had the climbers been more experienced, or had they hired a guide, this accident probably would not have happened.

The three horrified climbers spent the remaining daylight hours carefully descending LeFroy's steep icy slopes to where Abbot lay. A week later, rescuers brought Abbot's body down to Lake Louise where it could be attended to. This was the first climbing death in the Canadian Rockies.

During the 1920's, the Canadian Pacific Railway owned three hotels which catered to mountain hikers: Mount Stephen House in Field, BC, Glacier House in Rogers Pass and Banff Springs Hotel. Railway officials saw opportunities for increasing the number of tourists. Accordingly, they hired experts from Switzerland to act as guides and as teachers in mountain climbing.

Lefroy and Victoria became popular challenges. In 1922, to encourage climbers onto these mountains, the CPR built a hut at what is now known as Abbot Pass. This was no mean feat at that elevation and before helicopter transportation. At one time, the highest man-made building in Canada, the Abbot Pass Hut is a welcome shelter to exhausted climbers at the end of a day. Today, mountain climbers and hikers have become so prolific, the Alpine Club of Canada, who has taken over the management of the hut, has a full-time custodian on hand, and now charges a fee for over-night guests.

There is a story that some weary climbers coming from the British Columbia side arrived at Abbot Hut in the dark. When they entered it, the door pushed against something soft, causing the lead man to say, "Shh, people sleeping." The climbers tip-toed in, silently found themselves a spot on the floor, rolled into their sleeping bags and went to sleep. When they woke in the morning, they found they had been sleeping beside a dead man. He had been killed in a climbing accident the previous day, and his buddies had gone to Lake Louis to get help in bring-ing him down.

Rocky Morin on Mount Edith Cavell

Digging a place to sleep
on the Skyline Trail

Abbot Hut

When Rocky, Pete and I woke and stepped out of the Abbot Hut in the morning, we walked into a fresh fall of snow. That ended our climb before it began. Climbing Victoria in the new snow was too dangerous to attempt. We were disappointed, but consoled ourselves by deciding to see new country by descending the Alberta side and coming out at Lake Louise .

We didn't know that this side is far more dangerous than the British Columbia descent. The chief hazard is a steep, icy, narrow funnel known by mountaineers as the Death Trap. Avalanches coming from Lefroy and Victoria crash without warning, smashing anything in their way. At many times of day and anytime of year, shards of ice or cottage-sized chunks of glacier can hurtle down onto the floor of the Trap. According to old time Swiss guide, Edward Feuz, the Death Trap is the most dangerous place in the Canadian Rockies. Anyone descending or ascending Lefroy from the Alberta side has to negotiate the Death Trap. The safest time is that time of day when there is no thawing going on above.

As we scuttled through this trough as quickly as we could, the term "Russian Roulette" came to mind.

In time we reached Lake Louise, and walked along its shores until we came to the chalet and scores of weekend holidayers. We were able to catch a ride back to our car where, the day before, we had caught the bus to Lake O'Hara.

**

In 1964, Cam was ready to attend the university in Edmonton. Simultaneously, I was offered a challenging opportunity in the same city. I took the job of organizing and heading up the first industrial relations department in Fiberglas Canada's Edmonton plant.

Nineteen

WINTER CAMPING

Only the mournful and spooky sound of the wind reached me.

Now I was farther from the bush than ever. Working in the petrochemical industry in a city made me feel even more estranged from the wholesome, unscarred outdoors. Despite such a switch in ideologies and life style, I stayed with Fiberglas Canada Limited for twelve years.

There were two reasons for this:

First, the work was challenging, interesting and dynamic. There were more jobs in western Canada than there were people to fill them. Employees left their jobs for little or no reason because they knew other jobs down the street were crying for someone to take them. With impunity, they hit the bricks in wildcat strikes, and initiated fruitless grievances and arbitrations. Biennial contract negotiations were always a drawn-out battle. On management's side, I played a major part in these confrontations. In addition to labour relations, I was deeply involved in training, personnel, plant safety, fire prevention and security. The job excited and challenged me.

The other reason for my remaining in the city was Dot's contentment there. We bought a house near Edmonton's river valley where we could walk the dog, ski and enjoy the beauty. I began jogging three miles in the valley before breakfast. Every day, I delighted in seeing animal tracks or the animals themselves: sometimes porcupines; other times, skunks, pheasants, grouse, deer or coyotes.

The family took every opportunity to get back to the bush on weekends, holidays and vacations, camping out even during the win-

The family in the morning after a good night's sleep

ter months. We bought a canoe and explored rivers, creeks and lakes.

One day, while looking around with some friends, we stumbled upon a small wilderness lake of great beauty. Its water was clear, warm and a delight to swim in; it was a wild area where fish broke the surface in quest for flies. We have photographs of our daughter, Nancy, feeding wild ducklings out of her hand while the mother looked on. We could hear the beaver slapping their tails in the water as we lay in our sleeping bags close by. The narrow lake wound among the low contours for about four miles, revealing beautiful scenes as we drifted along in the canoe. It was hidden away from public view, and there was no proper road leading to it. After a heavy rain, the gumbo made wheeled access to it impossible. Always our favourite lake, we spent many weekends there. For ten years we were most often the sole visitors to this lonely spot until people in big boats with 50 horsepower outboard motors discovered it.

Nancy, getting
ready to leave
for home

Koko, our Boxer, found it tough
going in the deep snow

We used the national parks as much as we could. By this time, Jasper's Marmot Mountain had ski lifts and groomed slopes. The family spent many weekends perfecting our downhill expertise. Some of my happiest memories are of our daughter, Nancy, and me skiing together.

In the spring of 1967, the Canadian Broadcasting Corporation (CBC) wanted a television series of ten programmes on scouting. They gave me and two other writers a chance to compete for the job of writing the script. Each of us was to submit his work, and they would choose the one they wanted.

During my research, I learned that a troop of boy scouts was to camp on top of a fire lookout mountain about 12 miles north of Hinton. Using a map supplied by the Edmonton scout headquarters, I decided to locate them, and camp with them to pick up the flavour of scouting.

At that time a visiting engineer from Fiberglas' head office was in town. This man eventually became president of Fiberglas. Having never been west of Edmonton, he wanted to see the mountains. I told him I would put him on the right track to Jasper if he dropped me off at the foot of the mountain on which I was to meet the scouts. He agreed, and we set off on a frosty morning. When we got past Hinton, we drove off highway 16 onto a rural road to the Entrance Trading Post. Then, following my directions, he turned the car's nose down a narrow, snow-covered track leading through a thick stand of trees to apparently nowhere. As the miles slipped by – miles on which there was no trace of other vehicles on the freshly fallen snow – his anxiety became obvious.

"Are you sure I'll get back to the highway by myself," he asked?

There wasn't enough snow yet to impede a car, but we were in the middle of an unseasonal cold snap. When we arrived at the foot of my mountain, and I opened the door, a blast of cold air hit my friend like a bite from the Arctic. After I waved him goodbye, he almost spun his wheels to get back as quickly as he could to ploughed highways and civilization.

I shouldered my pack and set off up the mountain. The top was a few miles away, and I kept myself happily moving along by thinking of the big fire and supper that would greet me on my arrival.

When I reached the summit, the daylight had gone. I looked for the scout camp in the dark, but no light from a warm fire greeted me. The air held no smell of steaks being fried over the flames. Instead of shouts and laughter, only the mournful and spooky sound of the wind reached me as it soughed through the guy wires holding down the Forestry lookout cabin.

Hoping there might be a stove and some firewood in the cabin, I groped my way over in the dark. But it was locked up tightly. I had no choice but to go to bed in the snow. Slithering into my two down sleeping bags (one inside the other,) I arranged my boots around my body so they wouldn't be frozen in the morning, and snuggled down; no part of me was out, not even my head. The inside of that sleeping bag became my whole world.

When dawn arrived, I poked my head out of my bag to look out far below me on a wide, wooded valley. Beyond that, mountain peaks marched in disorderly ranks. The scene was wrapped in silence. What beautiful, peaceful solitude!

Building a fire, I warmed my feet, and thawed out my camera. I had to swing it back and forth over the flames for a few minutes before it would work. Between ice crystals in the air and the changing light however, I never did capture the beauty that had thrilled me at early dawn.

Picking up my pack, I set out for home. I thought I could reach Highway 16 in about six hours of walking. If someone driving east on the highway picked me up, I could stay overnight with Rocky Morin in Hinton until Dot came for me, or I got a ride back to Edmonton.

I no sooner got to the foot of the mountain than I experienced one of those occurrences that are so rare one finds himself talking about it years after. A World War 11 Jeep came bouncing through the snow towards me. In it was Al Bennet. Al had run the forest ranger district two districts south of mine in the Crowsnest Pass. I had not seen him since I had left Lynx Creek 18 years previously. Now an instructor for the nearby RCAF survival school, he told me the school officials had advised the scouts not to go up the mountain because of the cold snap. Instead, they had camped in a wooded valley a few miles away. Al dropped me off, and the scout leaders fed me a large breakfast. Later, I rode back to Edmonton with them.

I didn't get the job of writing the script on *Scouting* for the CBC. It was awarded to someone else.

A week or so later, I took Dot, Nancy and Jim to the top of the same lookout mountain. Unable to get our car to the foot of the mountain without chains, we had to return to the trading post at Entrance, and borrow chains from Gordon Watt, the owner. Gordon had been a ranger when I was in the Forestry, and I knew him well.

That night we camped like Indians on a spruce bough mattress beside a wood fire in a "wickiup" shelter. The word "wickiup" is of Algonquin origin, and is a shelter of conifer branches built in the shape of a small lean-to. While constructing it, we made a mistake that any experienced wickiup builder would never make. The entire weight of the hut is supported by a crossbar tied between two trees about five feet up the trunks. Instead of cutting a green pole, we used a dry one that had been lying on the ground nearby. Just as we

To get closer to the foot of the mountain, we had to put chains on the station wagon. Dot is watching.

completed our shelter, the crossbar broke with a crack. We watched unbelievingly as the entire structure slowly sagged to the ground.

After rebuilding the wickiup, we had a restful night, each in his/her eiderdown sleeping bag and with a big eiderdown robe over all of us. We dozed off watching the campfire flames die and the embers slowly go black.

Dot, the early riser among us, woke first. As she lay there, she was puzzled by a low moaning sound in the distance. The sound got closer and closer, and then suddenly we were hit with wind and snow.

Although the storm didn't bother us in our sleeping bags, we knew we had better get out of there quickly or we wouldn't be able to move the car waiting at the foot of the mountain. We were especially thankful for Gordon Watt's tire chains.

**

In 1968, Cam received his mechanical engineering degree, and promptly took off on a 2- year, 3- month trip around the world. He hiked through New Zealand and Australia, across Indonesia, in Japan, down to India, across Europe and home to marry his childhood sweetheart.

Meanwhile, after a year of university, Jim decided to look around for a rural lifestyle, and ended up among the Gulf Islands, living on a small sailboat.

Twenty

SPATSIZI COUNTRY

We were in the fabled land of the "red goat."

In 1976 I sensed it was time to move on from Fiberglas. It wasn't that things were going badly. Perhaps they were going too well. I had turned 55, and felt the need for another fling at life before I had to "shut her down". For a full year, I bounced back and forth between the "sensible" decision to stay put in a well-paying, secure job versus the chance to taste the thrill of venturing again into the unknown.

Both Dot and Cam's wife, Karen, encouraged me to take the big step.

I had a few things going for me. I was lecturing one night a week at the Northern Alberta Institute of Technology (NAIT); I had a seat on the Board of Referees (Unemployment Insurance Commission); I knew the government would award me the occasional contract to chair arbitrations and conciliations; I had received a commission from the provincial government to write a book on the history of the Alberta Forest Service, and I had a contract from the University of Alberta to teach a night course on the administration of the collective agreement.

So I thought I might step into the waters with these types of life preservers, and let the current take me from there.

The year 1976 was the start of a brand new lifestyle. No more regular hours; no more supervisor; and I wore blue jeans as much as I wore a suit.

Meanwhile, I lucked out. Sometimes I wonder if there is a guardian angel rescuing me from potential headlong collisions that I seem to hurl myself and my family towards.

I had phoned Grant MacEwan Community College (GMCC) to ask if they might have occasional work for an instructor. They told me they had just landed a large contract with the City of Edmonton, and were taking on contract instructors immediately. I attended an interview, and was hired as a result of my experience as a wartime army instructor, my lecturing at NAIT, and my industrial relations skills.

Through the months and years, more jobs came from new sources. I was working for the Continuing Education Division of NAIT, GMCC and the university. Then the provincial and federal governments and industry offered me 3-day and 5-day contracts.

Although harried at times, I loved the life. I liked working at home in my office developing lesson plans. I enjoyed the irregular hours, sometimes working part way through the night and sleeping in the next morning. I took delight in lecturing adults, although I would never have been a good schoolteacher. I liked the variety of subjects I lectured on, which included Employee Relations, Letter and Report Writing, Interviewing, Performance Appraisal, Delegating, Employee Discipline and others.

A huge benefit to my new lifestyle was the many times I got back to the bush. There would be a week or even a month when I had no commitments. Dot and I bought a 1/3 acre lot near Lac St. Anne, west of Edmonton, and only 3/4 of an hour's drive from our house. Absentee owners held the property on both sides of us for a long way. So we were almost in semi-wilderness. On it we built a little cabin, and used it for luxurious winter camping. So small was the cabin there was no room for a bed, only a place on the floor to lay out our foam mattresses. We built a tiny table under the window. The combination cooking and heating stove was a medium-sized tin airtight heater of a type known by every trapper and prospector.

I look back with great pleasure on waking up on a frosty winter morning, and still in my sleeping bag, sitting up to stuff some kindling and small wood in the heater, touching a match to it and sinking back in cosy comfort beside Dot while the fire warmed the cabin. Then later Dot filled the room with the delicious aroma of frying bacon and eggs.

Not far from us was an old historic railway line from which the tracks and ties had been removed. Now it was a trail through the bush. Other trails, meadows and ancient roads abounded in the vicinity, and the whole area was superb for cross country skiing. Going out on our skis, with no one else around, and roasting our sandwiches at noon over a fire was an activity we'll always remember.

**

In 1977 guide and outfitter Larry Erickson asked me to become an "evaluator" of an experiment he had in mind.

"I want to run the longest wilderness trip on the North American Continent," he wrote. "I need two outdoorsmen to evaluate a trial run for me. Will you be one of them?"

Although Larry was paying expenses, it would still cost me in lost business. However, I couldn't turn it down. I accepted immediately, and we left by aeroplane from Smithers in northern British Columbia on September 9th, Dot's and my 34th wedding anniversary.

The de Havilland Otter flew below the mountain tops, the wing on my side seeming almost to brush the rock. Leaving checkered brown and green farmlands, we were flying into a countryside of twisting canyons and high plateaus with an endless panorama of mountains rippling in all directions. Beneath the purple and brown peaks were open bunchgrass meadows and huge moors. Glacial and snow-fed streams appeared like shining silver threads making their way through the homeland of bears, wolves, and stone sheep that had seldom, if ever, seen man.

After an hour, we reached the headwaters of the Finlay, Peace, Stikine, and Skeena Rivers. A half-hour later, we landed on the partially constructed right-of-way of the Dease Lake extension of the British Columbia Railroad. This evidence of man's ambition to conquer nature rudely jarred me from my enjoyment of hundreds of miles of pristine nature. The raw gravel roadbed was like a scar across a pretty woman's face.

We were in Spatsizi country, the fabled "land of the red goat", 240 air miles north of Smithers. The area is so named because the local mountains contain a red iron ore dust in which the mountain goats roll, causing their white hair to become tinted. The Sikanni Indians called the area Tspah for the goat, and Tsize for red. This eventually became Spatsizi (spat-zee-zee) after which Spatsizi River and Spatsizi Mountain are named.

We were to begin a 200 mile 18-day pack trip by saddle horse from the Klappan River at the foot of Cartmel Mountain, east of Eddontenajon on the Stewart-Cassiar Highway. Our trip was to take us south-east through the Eaglenest Range across the Spatsizi River to the Stikine Range, through huge Spatsizi and Tatlatui Provincial Parks to Thutade Lake. This route traverses one of the few remaining large mountain wilderness areas in Canada.

The other "evaluator" was Ed McLarney, editor-publisher of the Skamania County Pioneer in Washington State. Ed was a tenacious moose hunter. The remainder of my travelling companions were: guide/cook Sue Sandeman-Allen and Burkhard Lepka, a young Austrian and Larry's general "go-fer."

Larry expected everyone to do his share in gathering firewood, fetching water, rounding up and saddling the horses.

The first few minutes of the first day almost finished the journey for me. I mounted a big grey gelding named Pat. For some reason, Pat began rearing repeatedly, standing on his hind legs and kicking into the air with his front legs. I made certain he had a slack rein, so I was not the cause of his strange behaviour. I sat there, expecting him to finally get sick of his 'horse-play' and move on. What I should have done was to have dismounted, got myself a stout stick, mounted again and given him a sharp rap on the skull. Finally he went right over backwards, landing on my legs, and pinning me to the ground. After much flailing of hooves, Pat got himself back on his feet, but I stayed on the ground, and asked the others to leave me lying there until the pain left me.

Finally, when I gave them the OK to help me, two of the men carried me over to Pat and put me back into the saddle. In retrospect, I can't imagine why they put me on the same horse, and I don't know why I let them. However, things went along well until we began climbing a steep bank. Pat got impatient at the delay caused by the packhorses up ahead and reared. His rear turned into a complete somersault on the sloping incline. I dived off in time to see him topple past me and roll over a second time, his neck bent under his body until I thought it had snapped. There he lay, still and – as everyone thought – dead. If I had not jumped at the time, the weight of the horse and the saddlehorn driven into my chest would have killed me.

To everyone's surprise, when Larry went to take the saddle off Pat, he lifted up his head, and eventually clambered onto his feet. After that I rode another horse, and Pat became a packhorse.

I was not able to walk properly for four days.

That first day was a tough one. Mostly bushwacking through balsam fir forests, we followed Eaglenest Creek alongside the Eaglenest Range of mountains. That night Ed hauled out his bottle of rum to give our tired spirits a lift. A disappointed shout indicated a problem in our anticipated refreshment. During the day's bouncing, the lid had loosened and the bottle spilled. From then on we always knew which packbox had held the rum. It never lost its ambrosial fragrance.

The next day we stayed in camp while Burgie rode out to scout a trail. I took the opportunity to climb part way up the foot of Mount Will. A few hundred feet above camp I sat and looked back over the country we had traversed the day before. It was majestic! A valley between two mountain ranges, the peaks white with fresh snow, and far below, our camp with tiny human figures, the bright orange canopy showing up like a splash of paint on the landscape.

Here were no stumps denoting an old logging operation; no wide, gravelled trails to take away the feeling of pristine wilderness; no other people on the trail or sound of cars in the distance; not even the exhaust trail of a jet plane.

The highlight of the trip was the Stikine Plateau in Spatsizi Provincial Wilderness Park. It was a long, tough climb. The horses worked their way uphill through an open pine forest. At the end of the timber, everyone dismounted and led his horse. Then for two and a half hours, horses and men scrambled up the steep mountainside. During the first hour, besides the steepness of the slope to contend with, was also an entanglement of dwarf birch catching at our feet and those of our horses.

The climb took us up almost 2000 feet, and I was thankful for the effort I had taken during the previous months to keep in shape. Although 20 years older than the next oldest in our group, I had no trouble keeping up. We were all glad to clamber at last over a lip and gaze onto a wondrous vastness. We were on top of the Spatsizi Plateau, a tableland of tundra as far as we could see. It was like standing on a ship in the middle of the ocean, and looking at nothing but water all the way to the horizon. It made me think of how the flatlands of Saskatchewan must have been before there were farms or fences.

I was surprised to learn that the tundra includes countless flowering plants, although we were too late to see them. The basic growth is the primitive lichen, a plant high in carbohydrates and most important to the foraging caribou.

One day, after descending from the plateau, we crossed the Stikine River at the site of an old Indian village called *Caribou Hide*.

Its history dates back to before World War I when a group of Sikanni Indians, fed up with the effects of the white man's whiskey and his treatment of them, broke away from the others. Packing their dogs with all their belongings, men, women, and children walked 150 miles through the mountains to the Stikine River. There they built their village on twin knolls.

They had been honest, hard working people, their integrity putting to shame the cynicism and materialism of much of today's world. Larry related that the Indians, near starvation, visited a white trapper to borrow some flour. The trapper was away, and the Indians helped themselves to a small amount of flour and lard, leaving behind furs worth many times the cost of the food.

Tragically, the band knew little other than hardship. At times they almost starved, and their numbers were decimated by croup and pleurisy. Finally, in the mid-30's, Chief Alex Jack and his councillors decided to move back to the protection of the white man's administration and paternalism, leaving a deserted village. It was these empty cabins we arrived at.

The next morning while Larry changed shoes on some of the horses, Ed and I visited the abandoned village. Lying beside the cabins, slowly disintegrating, were snowshoes, children's sleds, sawbuck packsaddles and wooden beds, all home-made by the inhabitants. The roofs on almost all the buildings were still intact, although the floors were rotten.

As I walked up the trail between the village and a small school, I imagined the kids coming home to their one-room log cabins. In the 1920s, I also had been attending elementary school, and was the same age as many of the Indian children. How different was my life from theirs', walking home on city streets to a six-room house.

A quarter mile from the village was a graveyard. On the edge of a high point of land overlooking Netsantan, it was solitary testimonial to the hunger, cold and disease that beset the Indians. Each grave was lovingly enclosed in a wooden fence with the corner posts whittled into ornate designs.

The simple inscription on one cross at the head of a small mound of earth summarised the hardship:

**Jennie died
May 18, 1933
2 year old**

When we left Metsantan Lake, we spent the first two hours on the old Toodoggone Trail (pronounced Too d'gon, the accent on the first syllable.) Its history dates to the 1930's and 1940's when up to a hundred horses in a pack train hauled commercial freight for mining prospects and settlements that no longer exist. One was the Hyland Trading Post near the junction of the Spatsizi and Stikine Rivers, long abandoned, but with its old building still standing.

Two days later we reached Lawyers Creek. All day we rode on wide moors where tiny lakes with no banks lay on top of the ground like drops of water on a leaf. Flat and treeless, the moors had a wild and desolate quality that reminded me of Sir Arthur Conan Doyle's book, The Hound of the Baskervilles.

That night we camped at Lawyer's Pass. It was named from the activities of Stuart Henderson, a Victoria lawyer who was involved in one of the most enduring legends of northern B.C. – that of Simon Gunannoot, a Sikanni Indian. In 1906, Simon and his brother-in-law, Peter Haimadan, were accused of murdering two white men. For 13 incredible years, in wilderness country north-west and north-east of Hazelton, Gunannoot eluded the best trackers in the B.C. Provincial Police. Even picked patrols, whose only duty was to find him, were unsuccessful. Finally he surrendered and was defended by Stuart Henderson, who won an acquittal for both Gun-annoot and Haimadan.

While living in the wilderness, Gunannoot had found some gold. After the trial he interested Henderson in going back to his old haunts to look for a possible mother lode. The wild and lonely stream they searched without success is now *Lawyers Creek*, its meandering path taking it through the pass we travelled.

On the 18th day, our journey ended at beautiful Thutade Lake. From there we hitch-hiked a ride on a hunter's float plane to Smithers, leaving Larry and Sue to ride the horses the rest of the way back.

**

Next year, in August, Dot and I camped for five days with about a hundred Skyline Trail Hikers four miles up Mosquito Creek in Banff Park. Although this time in the mountains was not nearly as physical as the Spatsizi trip, it had its own rewards. Each day we all divided into four or five groups according to our abilities and desires to hike in high country. Dot was content to be in the most relaxed group. They spent their days on the more gentle climbs and walking along the valley floor admiring and taking pictures of the many beautiful plants. The group I was in was the most active. We picked very high, tough hikes and scrambles, and were always the last ones back in camp in the evenings.

My morning pre-breakfast jogs at home had got me into good shape, and after the third day, I was asked to become a leader. I took my party on easy rock climbs, but without ropes. This was the first time any of them had scaled rock in which three points of contact were required for the sake of safety (i.e.both feet and one hand, or both hands and one foot on the rock.) According to one man, an Edmonton doctor, those were the best hikes of the week. The biggest thrill for me occurred one day when I looked down hundreds of feet below onto Dot's group. After much shouting, we attracted their attention, and through binoculars, I could see Dot waving.

The horse trip, the climbing, the hiking – these were the opportunities to get back to the bush that my new lifestyle had given me.

packing into the Spatsizi

TWENTY-ONE

THE LAND

Here we camped for thirteen months.

The Spatsizi trip encouraged my yearning to live in a wilderness setting on a full-time basis.

In 1979, after a thorough search for the type of property we wanted, we bought 30 acres on the shores of Lower Arrow Lake in British Columbia's West Kootenays. Simultaneously, our son, Jim and his family, bought the 30 acres next to us, built a house, and moved there from the coast.

The land was a large piece of wilderness with no roads or buildings on it. We had never seen a more beautiful spot... wooded mountains and deep draws against a backdrop of sparkling, transparent water.

The area embraced the solitude we were looking for. Our nearest neighbour, a mile north of us, was a jovial bachelor who made his living creating boutiques. To the south, a couple on the lake lived four miles away, and no one after that along the beach for about 30 miles. All the land between was either Crown land or possessed by absentee owners. Across the lake lived only one couple. More often than not, when we were on the lake, our canoe was the only boat within sight.

Four miles north-east of the land was a tiny hamlet and post office named *Fauquier* after a long dead pioneer of the area. Thirty-five miles farther north, the village of *Nakusp* is where we did our shopping.

In the spring of 1983, leaving our furniture and most of our belongings in storage, we moved to *The Land*, as we now called it, to begin the construction of our house. On the highway, passing motorists took a second look at a jam-packed pickup truck containing two people towing an equally jam-packed VW Bug with a huge German shepherd dog behind the wheel.

Near our proposed house site, a pleasant little opening of flat ground surrounded by cedars was where we set up our tent. During the early nights we lay in our sleeping bags enjoying the serenade of the frogs' chorus, the evening croaking of the ducks, and the eerie cry of a loon. Adjacent to the tent, Jim and I built a screened cookhouse, 10 feet by 15 feet – a home-made gazebo in effect – to make camping a little more comfortable.

Here we camped for 13 months. Dot loved cooking in the little cabin, fixed up with a long counter for her to work on. The screened walls gave her the feeling of being outdoors, and her view from every side took in cedar, Douglas fir, birch and larch. To the west she could see the lake, and also watch the house going up. For the winter we tacked plastic over the screen for warmth.

As *The Land* had no vehicle access, travel to Fauquier for mail, shopping and church was by canoe. Until we put in a driveway, we floated our lumber in by towing it behind a borrowed boat, powered by an 18-horse outboard motor.

The next year we hired a bulldozer to carve a road out of the bush. At 1 1/3 miles in length, it might be the longest private driveway in British Columbia and precipitous enough to make a goat look twice before descending it. In comparison, on most government highways, an 8 percent grade is considered to be steep; on a logging road, a 15 percent grade is a steep one. Our driveway contained slopes with a 20 and a 25 percent grade. The driveway remained a 4WD access, particularly in the winter. With the east part of it 500 feet higher than the west, we have enjoyed spring at one end while experiencing winter at the other.

To refer to any part of the driveway, we named each of the seven switchbacks, some after family members, and some through incidences that occurred at those locations. *Jacknife Hill* is where our utility trailer jackknifed when I attempted to pull it up the hill. We named *Bear Corner* after an incident with a bear cub.

No vehicle, not even a 4WD, could climb those slopes in the

winter unless we had a plough to take the snow off. We needed a tractor with a snow plough, and to get the rest of the lumber for the house down the hill as the lumber trucks were not about to risk the steepness of our new road.

A Kubota, 35 hp., 4WD with a snowplough and a front-end loader filled both needs. During the winter, I found it necessary to chain all four wheels. Each rear chain, with heavy lugs welded to it, weighed 90 pounds.

We had plenty of help to build our house. Taking control of the carpentry, our younger son, Jim, spent many days with me on construction. Our older son, Cam, became the electrician, and our daughter, Nancy, troweled the new concrete foundations. I was combination foreman, labourer and "go-fer." Dot was camp cook.

In May, we installed the septic field, hiring a backhoe to dig the trenches and hole for the tank.

That fall, we accepted an offer on our Edmonton house, and set out to drive back to Edmonton to make it available to the new owners. On our way there, we crossed the lake at Shelter Bay about 11 p.m., and decided to pull into the government campground there for the night. Dot slept in the cab of the truck while I lay crosswise in the cargo area next to the tailgate with the tailgate window open. In the wee hours of the morning I awoke to find a man standing over me with a bottle in his hand.

"What do you want?" I asked, looking up at him.

"I just want to talk about brotherly love." he said, obviously drunk.

"Not interested. Look for someone else." I replied.

He refused to move on even after my pleas turned to threats. I put on my shoes, got out of the truck and grabbed his arm that held the bottle. After a struggle, I gained possession of it, and threw the bottle as far as I could into the bush. From the cab, Dot, in amazement, watched her husband engage in a moonlight boxing match with a strange, unkempt looking man.

She quickly unlocked the door on the driver's side. I placed a well-aimed kick that stopped the intruder long enough for me to close the tailgate, jump into the cab and drive away.

As we were rolling along the road towards Revelstoke, I

said, "If that guy and his buddies decide to overtake us on this lonely road, we're in trouble."

I had barely said this when I noticed lights in my rear-view mirror quickly overtaking us. As we had come across the lake on the last ferry before the ferrymen went on strike, we knew it couldn't be any fresh traffic from the other side of the water. It must be the frustrated midnight reveller and his buddies bent on revenge.

"If they pass us," I said, "they can easily stop us." Dot nodded, but said nothing.

I stepped up the speed as fast as I dared go on the winding, narrow road, but the car quickly caught up. Whenever the driver attempted to pass, I prevented him by swerving from side to side.

"If we can get to Revelstoke," I said, "I'll drive at a high rate of speed up and down the streets until a police prowl car intervenes."

When we reached Revelstoke and pulled onto a street, the car shot passed. Instead of a gang of thugs looking for revenge, the car contained a boy and a girl who had been parked somewhere on a side road. He was probably rushing to get her home by a certain hour.

In November, Dot and I moved out of our tent into the new house, despite no doors or windows. What we gained in comfort, we lost in the alienation from the sounds, smells and sights of God's creation. In the house we noticed an immediate separation from these sensuous pleasures.

The mornings saw us racing in our pyjamas, kimonos and gum boots through the snow to the cookhouse (the screens now covered with plastic) to light the little tin heater that quickly glowed red and warmed the inside.

The temperature, more moderate than what we were used to in Edmonton, hovered between -10c and -15c. Every morning I had to chop a hole in the ice of our water trough.

We ended 1983 by working. On the morning of New Year's Eve, we got up early by the alarm to get more work done. That night, we went to sleep with the radio on, and the midnight revelry over the air woke me. Turning to wake up Dot, I wished her a happy new year.

Eventually, we finished the house. The kitchen, dining room and living room were one big room, 40 feet long and separated by waist-high sideboards. With large windows on every outside wall, we could see natural beauty wherever we looked.

Dot cooked by wood on a large kitchen range, and we heated by wood with a small heater upstairs and one downstairs in my office. Fuel costs consisted of two or three cans of gasoline each year for the chainsaw.

For a few years, obtaining water was a problem. There was no use drilling a deep well as we had no electricity to pump up the water. All we could do was dig a shallow well to bedrock, and pipe the seep water to the house. During the latter part of the summers our well dried up completely, and we had to catch rain from the house roof into the water trough. In winter we brought snow into the house to melt. Eventually, using the help, expertise and talent of my neighbor, a cement aficionado, I built a ferro-cement "tower" 100 lineal feet and uphill from the house. Being at a higher elevation, the water from our well flowed into the tower. When that source dried up, I pumped from the lake with a gasoline pump. The water from the 3000-gallon tower flowed to our house by gravity.

At 2:30 one morning in January, I awoke to noises indicating someone in the front room was turning over in his sleeping bag. I listened to these sounds for a minute before surmising that some of our relatives or friends had surprised us with a visit. Arriving late at night, and not wanting to wake anyone, they probably had put their bedding on the floor. I got up, happily anticipating a guest, and was disappointed to find no one in the house but Dot and me. Continuing to listen to the sounds as they occurred inter-mittently, I learned they were caused by small areas of snow ava-lanching off our steep steel roof.

Since then we often heard either the soft swish of a small snowslide leaving the eaves, or the roar followed by a thud as a large, heavy chunk broke off and thundered down the roof with enough force to kill a cat.

**

The summer of 1985 was the year of forest fires. The fires didn't threaten only our area; the town of Canal Flats was evacuated, and there was talk of evacuating Kimberly. At *The Land* a continual smell of smoke permeated the air. To the south of the house, smoke was drifting from fires on the other side of the lake. To the north of us, two fires burned near Fauquier, and across the lake were innumerable spot fires – so many it seemed the whole mountainside was on fire. Around our house, the view was hidden by a white curtain many feet high, its skirts touching the water.

One day I took the canoe south to look for new fires on our side of the lake. I found myself travelling in a "room" with milky walls that seemed to move along with me.

Three and a half miles farther on, I broke out of the heaviest part of the smoke, and came opposite to Potockis' property. I could see their house, which appeared in the smoke to be floating a few inches off the ground. South into the hills, smoke sat lethargically like some monstrous miscreation with its tentacles reaching into every draw.

On the way home, the once-familiar shoreline looked strange. Out of the smoke appeared cottages that had not existed before, and which turned into rocks or bluffs as I got closer. Finally, through the smoky mist appeared the empty deck chair Dot had been sitting on when I had left, and I knew that was the beach I was looking for.

In 1988, the problem of getting their children to school made Jim and his wife decide to move out. Dot and I lived there alone for nine years after they left.

We enjoyed eating outside, summer and winter. Sometimes, we lit a fire in the fire pit near the house. Other times we dressed warmly, and sat on our back or front decks. From the back, we looked out onto trails leading into the forest, and our narrow driveway winding down to the tractor shed. From the front deck we gazed for many miles down the lake where wilderness ravines unfolded between lofty wooded hills. At the far end of our vista, a princely range of rocky, prominent mountains was often covered with snow.

On some winter days, we snowshoed to a lonely shore where we lit a fire. During the spring, summer and fall we went in the canoe to one of the many nearby wilderness beaches, all of them uninhabited and unapproachable by land vehicles. On almost every beach was a supply of driftwood for burning.

Once, our grandson, Glen, and I camped on a lonely beach three miles south of the house and across the lake. That night we watched the three-quarter moon rise above the mountain peaks. It was a sight I had to show Dot, and a few nights later, we left by canoe. The weather was perfect: warm, calm and a clear sky. After we put up our tent, we sat for a while on a windfall in inky blackness looking eastward. About eight p.m. we watched a faint orange glow that quickly became more distinct until the edge of the full moon peaked above the mountain. Then gradually it rose behind the summit in all its grandeur, filling the valley with a silver light, throwing moonshadows into the trees behind us, and bright light on the sand in front. The melodic call of an owl in the woods put the shine on a magnificent evening.

Next morning when we were having breakfast under a bluff, we heard a strange sound. Climbing up to the open flat at the top of the bluff, I saw Heidi, our German Shepherd, running full speed towards me. On either side of her was a coyote, both of them trying to drag her down. A shout from me sent the coyotes on their way. Heidi loved to chase coyotes, and usually her good sense told her how far she should go, but this time she ran into more than she could handle.

Our most dramatic experience with wildlife happened when a full-grown cougar suddenly made an appearance. Had Heidi barked, the animal would have taken off into the trees. But she silently ran towards the cougar. The cat bounded towards Heidi in leaps that must have measured 15 feet in length. It all happened in a blur, and we had no time to call Heidi back. In a second it had the dog in its grip, and her screams indicated her shocked alarm. I ran, shouting, towards the big cat, who then dropped its prey and retreated into the bush. Heidi got away with a tear in her chest that took eleven stitches to close.

Another wildlife adventure almost as dramatic occurred at the switchback we subsequently named *Bear Corner*. It was here I ran into a small black bear cub. It looked at me benignly, but this didn't stop the icy fear from coursing through my veins.

Where is your mother, you little varmint?

Should I continue on my way or should I go back? Is she ahead of me or behind me?

A sound like a hoarse expulsion of breath told me she was ahead of me, and perhaps not pleased at finding me conversing with her cub. She was standing on her hind legs to study this intruder more clearly.

Bear books say, "Don't run. Stand your ground, even if the bear charges; it's probably bluffing." I wasn't able to run even if the idea did cross my mind. I was frozen to the spot. In retrospect, I don't think she was belligerent – just curious. Suddenly from out the bush Heidi, barking furiously, circled the bear. Bruin turned and climbed a tree. Calling Heidi, I immediately left.

**

Living in the bush gave us the opportunity to see nature in the raw. One winter day while Dot was looking out our dining room window, a hawk appeared directly below. Pushing its beak into the snow, it pulled out a struggling, luckless mouse. I had thought a hawk would tear a mouse apart as a cat does, and eat it in small bites. But this bird swallowed the mouse whole. It gulped many times, stretching its neck, and with each gulp the mouse slid down a little more.

Another time we watched a gull dive onto the surface of the lake to snatch a floating bug or piece of fish from under the beaks of two female coots (mudhens) that were just about to pick up the delicacy. Before the gull could become airborne, the coots jumped on its back and head, forcing its head into the water and held it there, apparently to drown the bird. The gull went limp. When the coots withdrew, the gull appeared to recover and attempted to fly away. But the coots, unforgiving, were onto the unfortunate bird again, pecking its head and forcing it under the water. This went on two more times until the coots finally allowed the gull to swim away. It seemed unable to fly by then, and swam towards us on the shore. Ignoring our presence, it climbed up the bank, and staggered into some tall grass.

A neighbour had an interesting experience one day with a hawk. She looked out her kitchen window just in time to see a Great Horned owl sitting on her pet cat. With righteous indignation and a great sense of urgency, she ran outside with her broom but came to a sudden halt when the owl met her attack with an unflinching stance.

Looking the farmer's wife squarely in the eye, the bird of prey emitted a fierce hiss. The woman uttered a Comanche yell and threw the broom at the owl, followed by her husband's gum boots and a milk pail, all of which were handy on the back stoop. The owl gave up in face of such an onslaught and flew away. But it was too late for the cat. When she got to it, it was dead.

In 1992, we installed two solar panels. The electric lights were a great addition to our lives. With an inverter, the panels gave us 24-hour, 115 volt (AC) electricity, although limited to lights only. From spring through summer and early fall, there was little need to run the generator to boost the battery. The sun did it all. In winter, we ran the generator to help out the sun, but only half as much as we used to. This saved us a great deal of gasoline money.

In 1995, *BC Hydro* agreed to give us power and to subsidise the cost of installing the 27 poles required to reach us. Hydro power had never been in our initial plans, but when we got it, we enjoyed its many benefits. We became spoiled with a freezer, a hot water tank and a computer. The biggest advantage was the electric pump in the lake that gave us water on demand. No more wrestling with my enemy, the temperamental gasoline pump.

In November of 1996, *BC Tel* allowed us a telephone. The wire lay on the ground for the entire 1 1/3 miles. It was a special wire, normally used for underground, and was more impervious to the gnawing teeth of mice than is the wire hung on poles. *BC Tel*, while good enough to sell us the wire, would not maintain it, however. The maintenance of our telephone line was our responsibility.

Then, in 1997, *BC Tel,* for a price, finally strung wire onto our power poles, and assumed responsibility for its maintenance.

**

Many people, knowing the hazards of our driveway, thought the "old couple" wouldn't last a winter out there.

The winter of 1997-98 was our 15th.

In the spring a young, adventurous couple from Germany offered us a fair price for our property. In our late seventies, Dot and I reluctantly but wisely accepted the offer.

On the night before we moved to Salmon Arm, BC, we stood on the front deck and looked at moon shadows sketched among the trees. The next morning, as we drove up the hill for the last time, I silently recalled some of our winter adventures on the steep driveway. When we reached Karen's Corner, "Brownie," the little brown bear that had been hanging around the previous week, crossed in front of our truck. We rounded Bear Corner and crawled up our old winter bogy, Jacknife Hill. I gulped, but said nothing to Dot. I knew her thoughts were the same as mine: "It's going to be tough living in town, but we'll adapt. We always have."

ISBN 155212404-5